Service Projects for Teens

20 Plans That Work

Compiled by
Tony Pichler
Chris Broslavick

Pflaum Publishing Group
Dayton, OH 45439

Service Projects for Teens
20 Plans That Work
Compiled by Tony Pichler and Chris Broslavick

Cover Design by Larissa Thompson
Cover Photo of "Youth Works" by Skjold Photographers
Interior Design by Patricia Lynch

Dedication

In Matthew's account of the Last Judgment, the Gospel writer tells us that "When the Son of Man comes in his glory, and all the angels with him, then he will sit on the throne of his glory. All the nations will be gathered before him, and he will separate people one from another as a shepherd separates the sheep from the goats" (Matthew 25:31-32). How will the people be judged? Scripture tells us that as we serve those who are hungry, thirsty, imprisoned, and lonely, we in turn serve Jesus.

This book, then, is dedicated to the Coordinators of Youth Ministry, Religious Education Administrators, and Principals in the Diocese of Green Bay, who serve Jesus by lending a preferential option for the poor, and, thus, model the Gospel imperative for the young people to whom they minister. Through the numerous service activities these leaders organize, they give the youth of the Diocese of Green Bay many opportunities to serve Jesus by serving others.

At the Last Judgment, Jesus will say to these dedicated men and women, "Come, you that are blessed by my Father, inherit the kingdom prepared for you from the foundation of the world" (Matthew 25:34).

Table of Contents

Introduction

For more than two decades, the Diocese of Green Bay, Wisconsin, has incorporated the component of service into its youth ministry and religious education offerings. Programs that served as early pioneers included the Diocesan Appalachian Outreach and Mississippi Outreach. In 1995, with the creation of Young Neighbors in Action, sponsored by the Center for Ministry Development, and Catholic Heart Workcamp, the diocese increased its awareness and activity surrounding the component of service. In recent years, as many as twenty-five parish and school groups have participated in national and regional service opportunities. Countless others have engaged the service component on a local level, serving in soup kitchens, clothing distribution centers, and housing rehabilitation projects.

When asked to compile projects to be published in this book, we asked for input from coordinators of youth ministry, religious education administrators, and school administrators throughout the diocese. From the submissions, twenty were chosen with the aim of offering a variety of service ideas for anyone working with teens. The result is this very practical and useful resource of successful service activities

The Pastoral Circle

In addition to being an already proven service project, each of these projects is also ideal for incorporating into the style of service learning called the pastoral circle. This process, adapted from the work of Peter Henriot and Joseph Holland, provides a vehicle for engaging young people in service opportunities. The process involves four distinct steps: involvement, exploration, reflection, and action.

The **involvement** stage connects young people to a social justice issue. Oftentimes, the issues are beyond the personal experience of most teens but are very real issues in the wider community. There are various ways to engage young people—to involve them—in a social justice issue. These strategies include the experience of an event (an experience of injustice), an issue (homelessness, environmental pollution, racism), a set of problems (economic and social decay in a neighborhood), or a question (Why is there a gulf between the rich and poor of the world?). Involvement helps to simulate the experience of a social issue. The ideas in this book can all serve as involvement experiences, stepping stones to wholistic service learning.

The next stage in the pastoral circle is **exploration**. This stage invites the young people to ask the question, "Why?" Why does this particular situation exist? What is the history of this situation? What is the future of this situation? The task at this stage is to examine causes, relationships, and structural realities to understand better the nature of the social issue and the avenues for change. Each activity in this book creatively leads to this point of the pastoral circle.

Reflection is the third stage on the pastoral circle. This stage engages the social issue in a conversation with the various sources of Church teaching, including the Scriptures, Catholic Social Teachings, and the resources in our faith tradition. The ultimate question is: "What does our faith say about this social issue?" Each project plan in this book supplies several Scripture citations and quotes from Catholic Social Teaching documents to begin this conversation between the young people and our faith tradition.

The fourth and last stage on the pastoral circle is **action**. After the young people have experienced the social issue through involvement, asked the "why" questions regarding its existence and future, and pondered the teachings of the Church about the issue, it is time for further action. Action is whatever process or project that the young people choose to help weaken or destroy the injustice they have recognized. The projects in this book can naturally lead the young people to "hunger and thirst for justice."

Helpful Features

Each of the activities in this book can be used as presented or modified to meet unique circumstances. You are the best judge of your group, your resources, and your community's needs. Nevertheless, in order to give you the most practical, straightforward help in using any of the projects in this book, the following format was used for each activity.

Purpose of Project—Following the title of each project, there is a brief description of the reason for the activity or the possible situation, circumstance, or season that might call for the activity. This information assists you in deciding if the project is, for example, an appropriate response to an international, national, or local disaster, a holiday youth-to-youth service activity, or a project to promote a specific cause, such as awareness of the needs of the elderly.

Scripture Reference—To firmly root the activity in *Church*, supporting scriptural texts are offered. These same texts are useful as starting points for initiating the development of the project, and/or they may be used for culminating reflections.

Catholic Social Teachings—The principles of social justice are provided for the same reason as the scripture references and have the same possible use.

Communities Involved—Activities may involve several unique groups without whom the project diminishes in effectiveness and meaning. If so, these groups are identified. Examples could include the senior class of a high school or religious education program, or parish families, or men and women of the parish who are serving in the armed forces. If such groups are not in your particular community, appropriate modifications of the project will be necessary.

Project Time Line—Successful planning includes mapping the events of an activity. Therefore, suggested time lines are offered. For example, the time line might suggest doing the project monthly from September through April, or using the activity during Advent or Lent.

Project Description—A narrative describes how each service project was developed and implemented. There is sufficient detail given to help you replicate this activity among most youth groups.

Special Considerations—If there are any contingencies, such as non-negotiable circumstances or the need for specific resources, these are identified as well. Examples of what those contingencies might be are that the parish or community have a food pantry, or that there be a long-term care facility within a reasonable distance from the parish or school.

Results—Comments are offered regarding the results experienced by the contributor when the project was carried out in his or her school or parish.

Reflection—The contributor offers his or her own thoughts on the project and suggests possible natural extensions of the project.

Remarks—Feedback from contributors, participants, and others, including those who were served, is included. The remarks often identify what could have been better or different, what went remarkably well and why, what cautions might need to be taken when doing the project, and how those involved felt after the project was completed.

Spreading the Word

The service component in the Diocese of Green Bay has exploded in the last two decades. It is our hope that as we share our ideas, experiences, and suggestions in this book, we will be helping you in your efforts toward a similar explosion in your own diocese, parish, or school, so that "this good news of the kingdom will be proclaimed throughout the world" (Matthew 24:13-14).

Clean Sweep

Designate and clean an area in your community on an ongoing basis for a three-month period. Reflect upon the experience through journaling.

And God said, "Let the waters under the sky be gathered together into one place, and let the dry land appear." And it was so. God called the dry land Earth, and the waters that were gathered together he called Seas. And God saw that it was good.

Then God said to Noah and to his sons with him, "As for me, I am establishing my covenant with you and your descendants after you, and with every living creature that is with you, the birds, the domestic animals, and every animal of the earth with you, as many as came out of the ark. I establish my covenant with you, that never again shall all flesh be cut off by the waters of a flood, and never again shall there be a flood to destroy the earth." God said, "This is the sign of the covenant that I make between me and you and every living creature that is with you, for all future generations: I have set my bow in the clouds, and it shall be a sign of the covenant between me and the earth."

The ever greater availability of material goods not only meets needs but also opens new horizons. The danger of the misuse of material goods and the appearance of artificial needs should in no way hinder the regard we have for the new goods and resources placed at our disposal and the use we make of them. On the contrary, we must see them as a gift from God and as a response to the human vocation, which is fully realized in Christ.

The knowledge that by means of work [we share] in the work of creation constitutes the most profound motive for undertaking it in various sectors. "The faithful, therefore," we read in the constitution *Lumen gentium*, "must learn the deepest meaning and the value of all creation, and its orientation to the praise of God. Even by their secular activity they must assist one another to live holier lives. In this way the world will be permeated by the spirit of Christ and more effectively achieve its purpose in justice, charity and peace."

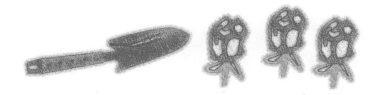

Pastoral Constitution on the Church in the Modern World [57] Vatican Council II, 1965

By the work of our hands or with the help of technology, we till the earth to produce fruit and to make it a dwelling place fit for all of humanity; we also play our part in the life of social groups. In so doing we are realizing God's plan, revealed at the beginning of time, to subdue the earth and perfect the work of creation; at the same time we are perfecting ourselves and observing the command of Christ to devote ourselves to the service of our sisters and brothers.

Communities Involved

Young people in grades 9-12, local governmental officials, and neighborhoods or parks in the local community.

Project Time Line

The actual clean sweep process is divided into two distinct parts: an intense period of cleaning followed by a maintenance program. The project begins in January and goes through September, as outlined in the Project Description.

Project Description

January

Recruit individuals to be on a Coordinating Team. This team should number no more than six individuals, both youth and adults. The role of this team is to select a clean-sweep site, work with local government officials, purchase supplies, recruit Clean Teams, and monitor the progress of the project.
Select a park or neighborhood in your community that needs cleaning.

February	The Coordinating Team contacts the local government officials to ensure their support for the cleanup of the selected site. If the site is a park, the city Parks Department or other governmental agency responsible for the parks in your area should be contacted. If the site is a neighborhood, contact the city planning office to ensure their support. Also, enlist the support of the residents in the neighborhood before the project begins.
March	After the site is selected and the proper permission is granted to begin the project, take a photo of the site before any cleanup begins. This photo helps give the group an indication of the progress they are making throughout the project.
April	The Coordinating Team recruits individuals to be on Clean Teams for the actual cleaning process. There should be four teams consisting of both youth and adults. Each team will clean the site one time per month.

The Coordinating Team purchases or arranges for the supplies needed for the clean sweep process. Necessary items include: gloves, garbage bags, trees/bushes (optional), rakes, shovels, lumber, and hardware for park benches (optional). |
| *May* | Coordinating Team determines a schedule for Clean Teams. Schedules are distributed to Clean Teams. |
| *June* | The first Clean Team thoroughly cleans the selected park or neighborhood. Following the clean-up process, each individual on the team journals what he or she has achieved. Each person should note his or her own perceptions of the task as well as any comments heard from neighbors or park visitors.

Each week, another Clean Team revisits the site and maintains the site. Teams may wish to plant flowers or bushes or build park benches during this time. Again, each individual should journal his or her perceptions of the task as well as any comments heard from neighbors or park visitors. |
July/August	Clean Teams return to the selected site on a weekly basis. The Coordinating Team monitors the work of the Clean Teams and replenishes supplies or secures any additional materials needed for the project.
Late August	Coordinating Team takes a photo of the site. Display both the Before and After photos in a prominent place in the parish.
September	Celebrate either a Eucharistic Liturgy or a prayer service on the site of the clean sweep to celebrate the accomplishments of the groups and to praise God for the gift of creation.

Special Considerations

It is imperative that approval by the local authorities and neighbors be gained before beginning this Clean Sweep project. If a neighborhood is selected for the project, it will be important to help the residents feel a part of the process. Visit with them. Invite them to join in the cleaning process. Also, invite them to the closing liturgy or prayer service to celebrate the completion of the project.

If flowers or bushes will be planted as part of the project, or if park benches will be constructed, it will be necessary to raise funds to cover these costs.

Results

The young people share their vision, creativity, boundless energy, and enthusiasm to beautify a park or neighborhood. The young people can more clearly see the beauty of God's creation. The young people will also build relationships with the residents or park visitors. If the residents are included in the process, an increased pride in the community can result.

Reflection

Young people who have participated in a Clean Sweep project, whether on a parish, school, or scout group level, have gained a greater appreciation for creation and for the Creator God.

Submitted by

Tony Pichler
Consultant for Youth Ministry
Diocese of Green Bay, WI

Clothes Vault

Purpose of Project

Provide appropriate clothing for unemployed women to wear for job interviews and to allow collaboration between a civic group and a youth group.

Scripture References

Matthew 25:37-40

[Jesus said] Then the righteous will answer him, "Lord, when was it that we saw you hungry and gave you food, or thirsty and gave you something to drink? And when was it that we saw you a stranger and welcomed you, or naked and gave you clothing? And when was it that we saw you sick or in prison and visited you?" And the king will answer them, "Truly I tell you, just as you did it to one of the least of these who are members of my family, you did it to me."

Catholic Social Teachings

A Call to Action, [48]
(*Octogesima Adveniens*)
Pope Paul VI, 1971

It is not enough to recall principles, state intentions, point to crying injustice and utter prophetic denunciations; these words will lack real weight unless they are accompanied for each individual by a livelier awareness of personal responsibility and by effective action. It is too easy to throw back on others responsibility for injustice, if at the same time one does not realize how each one shares in it personally.

On Human Work [26]
(*Laboreum Exercens*)
Pope John Paul II, 1981

The basis for determining the value of human work is not primarily the kind of work being done, but the fact that the one who is doing it is a person. The sources of the dignity of work are to be sought primarily in the subjective dimension, not in the objective one.

Communities Involved

High school youth group, a local women's advocacy group, and women seeking employment.

Project Time Line

Students collect and organize clothing for the Clothes Vault during the summer. The women's advocacy group continues with the Clothes Vault as an ongoing project.

Project Description

In the spring, assemble a team of students who will act as the core leadership of this project. Have your core team visit the offices of the advocacy agency to talk with the director and some of the clients. Have the advocacy group prepare a space to be used as the Clothes Vault.

Schedule clothing drop off times throughout May, June, and July. Have members of the core team and other youth volunteers accept donations and extend their appreciation to donors. Have clothing laundered or dry cleaned as necessary.

Special Considerations

The cooperation of a local advocacy group is essential. They can use their connections in the community to conduct a public awareness campaign to solicit donations. They can also advise other churches, shelters, and agencies about the creation of the Clothes Vault.

Results

Students met more than twenty-five donors and prepared more than six racks of outfits. They coordinated clothes with accessories like purses, shoes, and scarves.

Some students continue to donate their time on an ongoing basis, and they look forward to receiving training to assist clients with their selection and fitting of garments.

Reflection

Working with a community group has brought students into the "real world" of community service. Another advantage of this arrangement is that it gives the youth a picture of how some career choices can lead to a life of service to others.

Remarks

A sophomore volunteer commented: "I was really surprised at how many people came and gave us large donations. I am very happy to be helping with such a great project. There are so many people who have done so much for the Clothes Vault. I'd like to thank them all for allowing me to be a part of it all."

Adapted from project by

Rose Adler
Catholic Central High School
Marinette, WI

Coin Challenge

Purpose of Project

A particularly effective short-term activity for raising funds for a charitable cause. During the duration of the activity, provide opportunities for the students to learn about the work of the charity and the people who are served by it. This is a good activity to use at some time during the Lenten season.

Scripture References

Matthew 25:37-40

[Jesus said] Then the righteous will answer him, "Lord, when was it that we saw you hungry and gave you food, or thirsty and gave you something to drink? And when was it that we saw you a stranger and welcomed you, or naked and gave you clothing? And when was it that we saw you sick or in prison and visited you?"And the king will answer them, "Truly I tell you, just as you did it to one of the least of these who are members of my family, you did it to me."

Catholic Social Teachings

On the Development of Peoples [23]
(Populorum Progressio)
Pope Paul VI, 1967

"If someone who has the riches of this world sees his brother in need and closes his heart to him, how does the love of God abide in him?" (1 Jn 3:17). It is well known how strong were the words used by the Fathers of the Church to describe the proper attitude of persons who possess anything towards persons in need. To quote Saint Ambrose: "You are not making a gift of your possessions to the poor person. You are handing over to him what is his. For what has been given in common for the use of all, you have arrogated to yourself. The world is given to all, and not only to the rich."

Communities Involved

School students, Student Council, parents

Project Time Line

Because of the intensity of this activity, the project works best when it is run for a short period of time, about two weeks. Nevertheless, it can be run for any period of time that works best for you (see Special Considerations).

The Student Council engages the student body in a coin challenge. Grade levels challenge one another, and each classroom keeps a tally of points. A penny equals one point; a nickel equals five points; a dime, ten points, and so on. Each classroom has its own collection container.

One classroom can "wipe out" points of another classroom by putting money (points) in an envelope attached to the first class' container. The points that are put in the envelope of an opposing classroom get *deducted* from that class' total.

For example:
If five classrooms participate in this project, each student has an option of putting coins in his or her own classroom container and/ or in the envelope(s) in the other four classrooms. So, a student who has fifty cents has several choices:

1) put the entire fifty cents in his/her own classroom container and increase that classroom point total by fifty points

2) put thirty cents in his/her own classroom container and five cents in each of the other four classroom envelopes, thus increasing his/her classroom point total by thirty points and diminishing the point total of the other four classrooms by five points each

3) put twenty-five cents in his/her own classroom container and twenty-five cents in the envelope of the classroom which is the leader in points, thus increasing his/her classroom point total by twenty-five points and reducing the point total of the leading classroom by twenty-five

4) put the entire fifty cents in the envelope of another classroom and reduce its point total by 50 points

The challenge is to not only collect the most money for your own classroom but to retain the most points. It becomes a real strategical contest to allocate the funds for each day so that your own class accumulates points while, at the same time, tries to take away points from other classes.

Set aside the same fifteen-minute period each day for the rally to take place. Class total points for each rally period should be reported to the office at the same time each day. Money is handed in when point totals are reported. Point totals start over each day.

During the two-week challenge, offer occasional incentives for the classes. For instance, the class with the highest daily total could be granted a non-uniform day for the following day. At the end of the two-week challenge, tally the daily totals for each classroom. Give the class with the overall most points a special award or privilege.

Special Considerations

This project works well when the intensity of the challenge can be maintained. In a school, it is best to do this project over a designated period of time, for example, two weeks.

In a religious education program or a youth group, it might be best to carry out the project each time the group meets over a designated period of time, such as each of the six weekly gatherings of Lent, or the four weeks of a particular month.

In every case, inform the parish of the young peoples' project and invite parish support. While the parish may not participate in the challenge, it can be a part of the greater purpose, which is to raise money for a particular cause.

The key to generating the most funds is to keep the excitement level high. Chart class or group daily progress. Display the chart in a public place within the parish or school community.

Results

Our students did this activity to raise funds for a mission in Honduras. We have approximately 450 students in our school, and they raised over $4,000 in two weeks. Teachers who volunteered in the mission took the money to Honduras and delivered it to the mission director. The students enjoyed the project, and they became very familiar with Honduras. Parents also became involved in the challenge with their support.

Reflection

Students have asked to do this again, and their interest in the mission has led them to consider sponsoring a child in Honduras on a continuing basis. They would have a more personal contact with the child through an exchange of photos and letters, in addition to raising funds for the child's welfare.

Remarks

This is not a difficult project to do. All students can be involved to the extent that they are able. It is fun, and it gets good results.

Adapted from project by

Sister Kathryn Klackner
Holy Family School
Green Bay, WI

Cookie Bake

Purpose of Project

A parish intergenerational project designed to maintain a connection to recent high school graduates, plus initiate or strengthen relationships between adult and teen parishioners.

Scripture References

Matthew 5:13-16

[Jesus said] "You are the salt of the earth; but if salt has lost its taste, how can its saltiness be restored? It is no longer good for anything, but is thrown out and trampled under foot.

"You are the light of the world. A city built on a hill cannot be hid. No one after lighting a lamp puts it under the bushel basket, but on the lampstand, and it gives light to all in the house. In the same way, let your light shine before others, so that they may see your good works and give glory to your Father in heaven."

Luke 21:1-4

He looked up and saw rich people putting their gifts into the treasury; he also saw a poor widow put in two small copper coins. He said, "Truly I tell you, this poor widow has put in more than all of them; for all of them have contributed out of their abundance, but she out of her poverty has put in all she had to live on."

Catholic Social Teachings

The Plan of Pastoral Action for Family Ministry: A Vision and Strategy [1] U.S. Bishops, 1978

Changing circumstances in today's world call for a new approach within the Church to pastoral service to families.... In view of this, a plan of pastoral action is needed so that a genuine renewal might take place in the family ministry of the Church.

Apostolic Exhortation on the Family [66] *(Familiaris Consortio)* Pope John Paul II, 1981

The changes that have taken place within almost all modern societies demand that not only the family but also society and the Church should be involved in the effort of properly preparing young people for their future responsibilities.

Communities Involved

Middle school and high school teens, parents, family ministry group, parish women's group, parish members at large, recent high school graduates.

September

Set dates for baking and packing cookies. Preferably, choose two days within the same week: one for baking and decorating the cookies, one for making cards and packing the cookies.

Post notices in parish bulletin about the service project. Let parents know that they will be contacted to obtain the address and e-mail of their son or daughter who has recently graduated from high school and moved into a new life experience, e.g., college, the military, a job. The parish would like to send them a "We Care" package.

Inform parish committees, ministries, and departments of the Cookie Bake dates, and solicit adult help to work with the teens. Emphasize that love for young people and lots of patience are needed. Each adult should bring the ingredients to mix and bake a batch of cookies.

Other supplies that are needed:

- frosting and cookie decorations
- donations for postage
- popcorn kernels to air-pop (unsalted) for shipping
- wrapped candies to use as filler in the boxes
- packets of hot chocolate
- gallon-size freezer bags for cookies (the zip-up type work best)
- boxes for shipping (Tip: Check with parish office for envelope boxes. That size works very well.)
- mailing labels
- paper grocery bags to use for wrapping packages
- shipping tape

End of September	Mail a form to the parents of the recent high school graduates. Ask that it be returned to the Youth Minister. On the form, include a place for the name of the recipient, school (if it applies), current mailing address, phone number, and e-mail address. Also, assign a return due date, and include a note that a follow-up telephone call will be made if the form is not returned. (Note: Expect the response to be good. Parents are usually very happy that the church is reaching out to their young adult!)
October	Begin advertising for volunteers among the teens by putting notices in the bulletin, hanging flyers and posters, making class announcements, and sending e-mails. Ask teens to sign a commitment form. This helps to plan for the correct number of adult helpers and to arrange the appropriate number of work stations. Include both work dates on the commitment form so they can choose one or both nights: the night for baking and decorating and the night for making cards and packing the cookies. Each night should take about two hours.
	Maintain an up-to-date list of the addresses and e-mails you are receiving for the young adults.
	Stay in contact with the other committees and ministries and ask for a commitment from the adults.
November	Make final checks on adult helpers and teen volunteers, and confirm any last minute recipients' addresses and emails.
	Prepare adult helpers by reminding them what it is like working with teens. Some teens may have never used measuring cups or helped bake anything before, so patience and an ability to work side by side with teens is important. The young people need guidance, but they should do a lot of the work themselves. Resist the tendency to pitch in and do it for them.
	Make sure there is enough equipment (mixers, bowls, cookie sheets, popcorn popper, measuring utensils, aprons, and so forth).
	Gather construction paper, glitter, markers, scissors, glue stick, rubber stamps, ink, and any other material you'll need to make cards.
	Finalize the list of names and addresses. As much as possible, include a note by each person's name giving the information about where they are and what they are doing, i.e., the name of the college they attend, or the branch of the military they are in, or what kind of job they have. It is also helpful to have a sample message prepared to help the card makers get started.
	Create a "prayer request" card to enclose in each package. It should invite the recipient to send their prayer needs back to the parish. Include a little message from the parish, along with the parish mailing address, email address, and website (if applicable).

If possible, arrange to have an instant-developing camera on hand. Designate someone to shoot candid photos of all the fun during the baking and packing. Then add a photo to the package so the recipient can see some of the action.

Night One   Baking Date—Welcome everyone. Explain to the whole group what is being done and why. Pray together. Assign groups of young people and adults and be sure introductions are made so the team members know one another. Be ready for wonderful things to happen.

Station adults at the ovens to keep things moving. Sugar cookies should be baked first so that they can cool and be decorated that same night.

If there are more teens waiting to be bakers, they can be assigned to air pop the popcorn or to begin making cards.

Limit the activity to two hours. Allow enough time within that two hours for clean up. Make sure the teens are involved in the clean up!

Night Two   Packing Date—Set up tables for the following activities:

1. A line of tables for cookies (1-2 dozen in each plastic bag), wrapped candies, hot chocolate packets, popcorn filler.

2. Table for making cards. Have card-making materials and the list of names at this table.

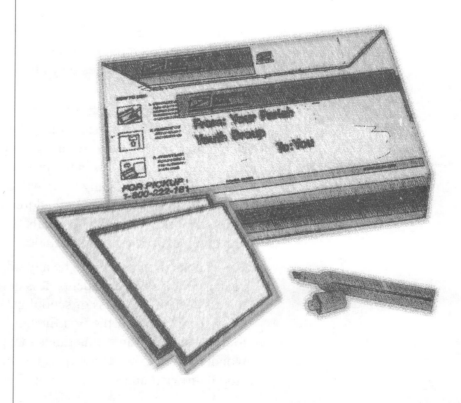

3. Table for completed cards, prayer request cards, message from parish, address labels/return address labels (Note: Make sure the address label matches the card inside the box.)

4. Table(s) for wrapping, sealing, and addressing the boxes.

Limit the activity to two hours, allowing for clean up.

Next Day   Take packages to post office. Ship regular ground mail for local deliveries. Check the cost for sending boxes to farther destinations. Often, priority mail is as economical as regular, or not much more costly.

Send thank-you notes to adult helpers and donors. Post a bulletin thank-you for all who helped. Add a photo or two, if possible.

Special Considerations

Frozen cookie dough may help save time—just bake and decorate, if necessary. If your parish facilities do not have enough ovens to bake all the cookies in one night, you might ask some adults to bake a batch of cookies at home and deliver on the packing day.

Results

Expected results   Parish connection with the young adults—homemade cookies, offer to pray for them, email addresses to maintain communication, teens reaching out to their graduated classmates. Grateful and surprised recipients.

Unexpected results   Very rewarding interaction between the teens and adults (adults are often grandparent age); new relationships building; teens learning from adults how to bake; both age groups attempting to communicate effectively; teens feeling very good about sending messages to the graduates they know from the parish.

Reflection

This has been a most successful service project for the parish. Being intergenerational, so many people are able to provide either time, talent, or treasure. In the process of sending a simple surprise "we-care" package, many other wonderful benefits have resulted. And, now that we have e-mail addresses, we can send messages throughout the year. Many e-mails from students have come back to us with expressions of gratitude.

Pre-Thanksgiving seems to be a good time of the year to send the package. For college students, it is near midterm exams and during the time when the stress of school gets to be high. For all who are away from home for the first time, it is nice to have this treat prior to the busy-ness (and sometimes loneliness) of the holidays. It was wonderful to have recipients who came home for Thanksgiving stop by to visit and say thank you.

Remarks

Parent of young adult: "It is just wonderful to do this. My daughter was so surprised!"

Teen volunteer: "This was fun! Are you going to do this when I go to college?"

Postal Worker: "What a thoughtful thing to do. I wish my church would reach out to my daughter in college."

Recipient: "Thank you so much for your prayer package! The card was beautiful and the cookies and candy were delicious! Thanks too, for your prayers. I'll pray for all of you too!"

Submitted by

Peg VandeHey
Coordinator of Youth Ministry
St. Thomas More Parish
Appleton, WI

Do-It-Yourself Food Shelf

Purpose of Project

Organize a parish-based food shelf using the human, material, and financial resources of the parish and its parishioners.

Scripture References

John 6:8-14

One of his disciples, Andrew, Simon Peter's brother, said to him, "There is a boy here who has five barley loaves and two fish. But what are they among so many people?" Jesus said, "Make the people sit down." Now there was a great deal of grass in the place; so they sat down, about five thousand in all. Then Jesus took the loaves, and when he had given thanks, he distributed them to those who were seated; so also the fish, as much as they wanted. When they were satisfied, he told his disciples, "Gather up the fragments left over, so that nothing may be lost." So they gathered them up, and from the fragments of the five barley loaves, left by those who had eaten, they filled twelve baskets. When the people saw the sign that he had done, they began to say, "This is indeed the prophet who is to come into the world."

Catholic Social Teachings

Communities of Salt and Light [3]
U.S. Bishops, 1993

Our parish communities are measured by how they serve "the least of these" in our parish and beyond its boundaries—the hungry, the homeless, the sick, those in prison, the stranger (cf. Mat 25:31). Our local families of faith are called to "hunger and thirst for justice" and to be "peacemakers" in our own communities (cf. Mt 5:6,9). A parish cannot really proclaim the gospel if its message is not reflected in its own community life.

Economic Justice for All [8]
U.S. Bishops, 1986

As *Catholics*, we are heirs of a long tradition of thought and action on the moral dimensions of economic activity. The life and words of Jesus and the teaching of his Church call us to serve those in need and to work actively for social and economic justice. As a community of believers, we know that our faith is tested by the quality of justice among us, that we can best measure our life together by how the poor and the vulnerable are treated. This is not a new concern for us. It is as old as the Hebrew prophets, as compelling as the Sermon on the Mount, and as current as the powerful voice of Pope John Paul II defending the dignity of the human person.

Communities Involved

High school teens and their families, friends, and acquaintances, as well as the rest of the parish community.

Project Time Line

This project can take only a few weeks or several months, depending on the complexity with which the food shelf is implemented.

Project Description

Organizing a parish food shelf involves several principles that will ensure the creation of a just and helpful resource for those people who need food and other material goods with which to survive.

Make the collection of resources a natural action of the parish. To achieve this atmosphere of giving, several homilies or reflections by the pastor or the young people of the parish may be necessary. Draw upon the Scripture and Catholic Social Teaching citations listed here for these presentations. The coordinator or committee should create reminder pulpit announcements and bulletin inserts as further reminders.

Devise a list of items that are needed for the food shelf. The list can be as simple as non-perishable food staples like canned fruit, vegetables, and soups. Or, it can be more extensive to include items like baby necessities, bedding and linens, clothing, perishable goods like bread and fresh fruit and vegetables, or common medical supplies like bandages and aspirin.

The list can be included in the parish bulletin or distributed after Masses.

Place no boundaries on the distribution of the collected goods. Keep the shelf in a location that is easily accessible. It is important that those in need should feel no shame in taking items from the food shelf.

Distribute goods with "no strings attached" and require that no paper work be completed in order to qualify for the necessary goods. Forms create a sense of bureaucracy that makes those in need feel a loss of self-esteem. Also, this bureaucratic measure will make the system of distribution more complicated and time-consuming for the parish young people. Operate with the motto: "Give what you can—take what you need."

Create a system for maintaining the food shelf. A coordinator or committee of young people can be recruited to oversee it. Encourage young people to volunteer one hour per month to organize and clean the food shelf. Items should be stored in bins or on shelves that are labeled for easy recognition.

Special Considerations

There is a need for a suitable space in the parish to keep a food shelf collection. The space should be easily accessible by both those in need and those who are donating goods. Shelves or boxes are also needed (large packing boxes work well). Decorate and label the shelves/boxes so the food shelf will be a welcome spot as well as a practical one.

Results

Involving the entire parish in this activity results in a broader feeling of ownership in the experience. Everyone can feel a part of the project, from the young people who organize it to the elderly who may not be able to help physically but can donate goods from their own blessings.

Reflection

There is no better way to personally bring to life the Gospel challenge to share, as exhibited in the multiplication of the loaves, than the creation of a food shelf in a parish. Whereas Jesus somehow persuaded those who brought bread to share their blessings with those in need on the hillside, parishioners are challenged to provide food and clothing to the needy by sharing their personal blessings. In the end, the reign of God is brought to completion more fully.

Idea contributed by

Reverend Marty Carr
Director, The Place 2B,
Oshkosh, WI

Feast the Hungry

Purpose of Project

Plan and serve a meal and lead a prayer service for the parish and wider community, including the poor.

Scripture References

Exodus 16:4-5

Then the LORD said to Moses, "I am going to rain bread from heaven for you, and each day the people shall go out and gather enough for that day. In that way I will test them, whether they will follow my instruction or not. On the sixth day, when they prepare what they bring in, it will be twice as much as they gather on other days."

Acts 2:42

They devoted themselves to the apostles' teaching and fellowship, to the breaking of the bread and the prayers.

Catholic Social Teachings

Economic Justice for All [170]
U.S. Bishops, 1986

More than 33 million Americans—about one in every seven people in our nation—are poor by the government's official definition. The norms of human dignity and the preferential option for the poor compel us to confront this issue with a sense of urgency. Dealing with poverty is not a luxury to which our nation can attend when it finds the time and resources. Rather, it is a moral imperative of the highest priority.

On the Development of Peoples [47]
(Populorum Progressio)
Pope Paul VI, 1967

The struggle against destitution, though urgent and necessary, is not enough. It is a question, rather, of building a world where every [person], no matter what...race, religion or nationality, can live a fully human life, freed from servitude...a world where freedom is not an empty word and where the poor man Lazarus can sit down at the same table with the rich man.

Pastoral Constitution on the Church in the Modern World [4]
(Gaudium et Spes)
Vatican Council II, 1965

Never has the human race enjoyed such an abundance of wealth, resources and economic power, and yet a huge proportion of the world's citizens are still tormented by hunger and poverty, while countless numbers suffer from total illiteracy.

Communities Involved

Young people in grades 9-12, the parish community, and the wider community.

Project Time Line

This activity can be done once, on a monthly basis, or a seasonal basis.

Gather a group of young people with the distinct purpose of "feasting the hungry" both with food and message. Use the following steps in your planning:

1. Set a date for the "Feast the Hungry" night.

2. Plan a menu. Consider a simple soup and bread for the main course. Cookies or bars can suffice for dessert.

3. Purchase the supplies necessary for the "Feast the Hungry" meal. (See Remarks.)

4. Advertise the "Feast the Hungry" dinner through various means. Announcements in the parish bulletin are a good start, but also consider placing registration slips in the corners of the pews. Posters with informational tear-off slips on the bottom can be distributed to area businesses and other points of interest in the community. Take advantage of public service announcements on the television and radio, and encourage everyone to "tell a friend." In all advertisements, a deadline for reservations is necessary for planning purposes.

5. Make enough copies of the Feast the Hungry prayer on page 30 for the participants. Recruit either a community member or a parish young person to provide a 5-7 minute witness talk in the context of the Feast the Hungry prayer. The presentation should address some dimension of social justice. Possible topics include hunger, homelessness, discrimination, or welfare reform.

6. On the night of the "Feast the Hungry" meal, the following schedule works well:

> 6:00-6:45 p.m. Meal
> 6:45-7:30 p.m. Prayer and Message

Special Considerations

Seek out a person as an advisor who has cooked for large numbers of people. This person will be able to translate a recipe for soup to the numbers of people that are expected for your meal.

The parish will need an ample kitchen equipped with the necessary utensils, dishes, cookware, and a dining room or cafeteria for the "Feast the Hungry" meal.

Results

People build community, not only within the parish but also within the wider community.

Reflections

Young people are the force behind an outreach to their elders in the parish and wider community. In the context of this meal, the young people can share with the community some insights on social justice and at the least raise awareness of the needs of the poor.

Remarks

Fund raising may be necessary to cover the cost of the meal, but also consider asking for donations either from the parish or business community. You could also ask participants for a minimal donation at the door on the night of the dinner.

Idea contributed by

Julie Massey
Pastoral Associate
St. Norbert College Campus Ministry
DePere, WI

Feast the Hungry

PRAYER SERVICE	
Presider	May grace, mercy, and peace from God and from Jesus Christ our Lord be with you.
All	And also with you.
Presider	Let us pray. Lord God, we are ever more mindful of the injustices that exist in the world. Enlighten our understanding and lead us in our efforts to eliminate oppression, hunger, discrimination, and every evil rooted in injustice. Hear us now as we pray for your presence among us tonight and always. We ask this in the name of Jesus, the Liberator and Savior of the world.
All	Amen.
PROCLAMATION OF THE WORD	Matthew 25:31-46
REFLECTION	*(At this time, a designated speaker will witness for 5-7 minutes.)*
PRAYERS OF THE FAITHFUL	
Presider	Confident that our God is faithful, we pray for the following needs. The response is, "Lord, be with us as we feast the hungry."
Reader 1	That both our church and civic leaders be a leaven of living hope for those who have little or none, we pray to the Lord...
Reader 2	That we, who are called to live generously and act justly, be a people of solidarity with the poor, we pray to the Lord...
Reader 3	That the work of our hands be a "yeast" that mixes and rises to become the much-desired Reign of God, we pray to the Lord...
Reader 4	That each of us may come to realize that the deep hunger within us can be satisfied only by God, we pray to the Lord...
Reader 5	That we may deprive ourselves for the hungry, and satisfy the needs of the afflicted, we pray to the Lord...

| *continued*

Reader 6 | That all of us who are members of the faith community here at *[name of parish or school]* realize that as baptized Christians we are called to pass on the faith to others, we pray to the Lord...

Reader 7 | We invite you to share your intentions at this time with this community gathered in the Lord's name.

Reader 8 | For the hungers we hold silently in our hearts, we pray to the Lord...

Presider | Loving God, give us the generosity we need to reach out to the physical hunger of those around us and to attend to the hunger for justice that each of us has in our hearts.

All | Amen.

Presider | And now we pray as Jesus taught us. Our Father...

All | (join in praying the Our Father)

Presider | Lord God, direct our concerns to the poor and oppressed of the world. Let us hear their voices as your voice. Give us strength to respond to your call and to reach out to our brothers and sisters. We ask this through Jesus, the Christ.

All | Amen.

Closing | Sing "Table of Plenty" (©1992 Daniel L. Schutte, Oregon Catholic Press) or another appropriate song.

Gathering with Elders

Purpose of Project

This is an activity that brings young people and older adults who are residents of a Nursing Home together for an evening of "fine arts."

Scripture References

Matthew 22:37-39

[Jesus] said to him, "You shall love the Lord your God with all your heart, and with all your soul, and with all your mind." This is the greatest and first commandment. And a second is like it: "You shall love your neighbor as yourself."

Romans 12:9-13

Let love be genuine; hate what is evil, hold fast to what is good; love one another with mutual affection; outdo one another in showing honor. Do not lag in zeal, be ardent in spirit, serve the Lord. Rejoice in hope, be patient in suffering, persevere in prayer. Contribute to the needs of the saints; extend hospitality to strangers.

Catholic Social Teachings

Blessings of Age [26]
U.S. Bishops, 1999

"We ask you to see ... older persons as God's gift to you and to the entire faith community, talk with them, learn from them, and draw inspiration from them."

Pastoral Constitution on the Church in the Modern World [27]
(Gaudium et Spes)
Vatican Council II, 1965

This Council lays stress on reverence for [the human person]; everyone must consider [one's] every neighbor without exception as another self, taking into account first of all [the person's] life and the means necessary to living it with dignity, so as not to imitate the rich man who had no concern for the poor man Lazarus.

Communities Involved

A group of young people and residents of a nursing home.

Project Timeline

This is an on-going project, but two months prior to the first visit, initiate a meeting of 15-20 interested students to plan the activities. Contact the nursing home to obtain permission for the visit(s).

Project Description

Plan a "fine arts" activity with the students that they can organize and run at an area nursing home. Some suggestions are arts and crafts, sing-alongs, one-act plays, and performances by students who play instruments or sing. The young people should take responsibility for providing any needed materials.

In advance of the event, always obtain the activity director's approval of the plans. He or she should also be present to assist in the activity.

On the day or evening of the event, gather 30 minutes early with the students to pray and to discuss last-minute preparations. After the event, remain another half hour to review the time together and to end in prayer.

Agree on a set date to do this each month, and have a different person be responsible for the opening and closing prayer at each event.

Special Considerations

The cooperation of an area nursing home is essential. There must be parents or other adults to assist and supervise the youth.

Results

Students become comfortable in the nursing home environment. Many of the students form lasting friendships with the residents, and the elderly people enjoy and look forward to the students' coming. All who are involved with this project benefit in some way from the experience.

Reflection

This project is a good way to get parents involved in a service project with their teenagers.

Remarks

One parent thought the project was an excellent idea because her daughter would probably not have chosen to visit a nursing home by herself.

The students began to form relationships with the residents. One young person "adopted" a grandmother whom he continues to visit.

Adapted from project by

Sarah Simon
Xavier High School
Appleton, WI

Meals During Lent

Provide meals for residents of a domestic abuse shelter. Most of the residents work during the day and take turns preparing the evening meal. Meals During Lent provides dinners twice each week throughout the season of Lent. This almsgiving project is initiated and coordinated by the teens in each family.

Jesus called to them and said, "It will not be so among you; but whoever wishes to be great among you must be your servant, and whoever wishes to be first among you must be your slave; just as the Son of Man came not to be served but to serve, and to give his life a ransom for many."

[Jesus said] "Beware of practicing your piety before others in order to be seen by them; for then you have no reward from your Father in heaven.

"So whenever you give alms, do not sound a trumpet before you, as the hypocrites do in the synagogues and in the streets, so that they may be praised by others. Truly I tell you, they have received their reward. But when you give alms, do not let your left hand know what your right hand is doing, so that your alms may be done in secret; and your Father who sees in secret will reward you."

There is a growing awareness of the sublime dignity of human persons, who stand above all things and whose rights and duties are universal and inviolable. They ought, therefore, to have ready access to all that is necessary for leading a genuinely human life: for example, food, clothing, housing.

Communities Involved

High school teens and their families, as well as other families in the parish.

Project Time Line

Meals During Lent is a ten-week project, which includes three to four weeks of planning and preparation, plus the six weeks of Lent.

Project Description

Several weeks before the Lenten season, introduce the idea to the teens in your high school religious education or youth program. The young people in this project are expected to engage their family's participation and to coordinate the preparation of the meals.

As a group, discuss the following:

- Decide which two nights of the week will be the Meals During Lent nights. (Tuesdays and Thursdays work well.)

- Develop some sample menus. Note: On any given night, all of the families should make the same meal. For instance, on the first Tuesday, the menu could be spaghetti, salad, french bread, and brownies. On the first Thursday, the menu could be baked chicken, rice, green beans, gelatin salad, rolls, and cookies.

- Make lists of ingredients that would need to be purchased or supplied by each family.

Establish a deadline of one week before Lent begins for having youth/families commit to a particular date. It works best if there are three or four families preparing meals for each of the dates. Leftovers are welcome if there are not enough residents to finish a night's meal. Make sure all dates are covered.

Write a letter to each family outlining what to prepare, for how many, where to deliver the meal, and other necessary details. Instruct families to mark their dishes and to return in two or three days to pick them up.

Unless families have concerns or questions, or want to sign up for additional days, no further contacts should be necessary.

Special Considerations

Most areas have a domestic abuse shelter or other shelters, so having a facility within driving distance shouldn't be too much of a problem.

Making contact with the facility or agency and maintaining confidentiality as requested needs to be stressed.

Designated teens may make reminder calls to families the day before their chosen meal preparation days.

Results

The appreciation of the residents at the shelter was the most notable result.

In some families, all the members worked together on the preparation of the meal; in others, the teen/s did everything. It was a very good experience for everyone, and we had a great response.

Reflection

We all know what it's like to come home after a busy and full day and have to prepare an evening meal. This project gave people who are already under extreme stress some welcome relief from this evening meal chore. It also allowed our parish members to reach out and share their gifts of food and time. Furthermore, this project promotes community (relationships that shape people) and cooperation (working with others toward a common goal).

Remarks

In our parish, several families who participated continued this project in their RENEW groups.

Submitted by

Meg Casey
Coordinator of Youth Ministry
Inter-Parish Religious Formation
Appleton, WI

The Mobile Church

Purpose of Project

Provide on-site prayer presence to the family and friends of victims of crime, accident, or other traumatic and untimely death.

Scripture References

Micah 6:8

And what does the Lord require of you but to do justice, and to love kindness, and to walk humbly with your God?

John 11:33-36

When Jesus saw her weeping, and the Jews who came with her also weeping, he was greatly disturbed in spirit and deeply moved. He said, "Where have you laid him?" They said to him, "Lord, come and see." Jesus began to weep. So the Jews said, "See how he loved him!"

Catholic Social Teachings

Pastoral Constitution on the Church in the Modern World [42] *(Gaudium et Spes)* Vatican Council II, 1965

Christ did not bequeath to the church a mission in the political, economic, or social order: the purpose he assigned to it was religious. But this religious mission can be the source of commitment, direction, and vigor to establish and consolidate the human community according to the law of God. In fact, the church is able, indeed it is obliged, if times and circumstances require it, to initiate action for the benefit of everyone, especially of those in need, such as works of mercy and the like.

Communities of Salt and Light [10] U.S. Bishops, 1993

Catholic social teaching more than anything else insists that we are one family; it calls us to overcome barriers of race, religion, ethnicity, gender, economic status, and nationality. We are all one in Christ Jesus (cf Gal 3:28)—beyond our differences and boundaries.

Communities Involved

This ongoing service can be offered to your own parishioners or extended into the community at large. This is a decision for your group to make. Young people, entire families, parish groups, and pastoral ministers can all participate.

Project Time Line

The timing of this project is governed by the needs of the community. Have on hand a prepared prayer service for the times you may choose to use one (see sample on page 41). Have copies available for distribution. Also, be prepared with an appropriate song, poem, or reading with which to conclude the service.

To initiate the program, establish a contact with the parish office and/or the local medical examiner or coroner. In addition, inaugurate a system for checking daily local newspapers and newscasts. These will be your sources for obtaining the names of victims and the locations of the crimes or accidents.

When word is received that a crime or accident has taken place, obtain the name of the victim(s), the location of the incident, and a phone number or name of a contact within the victim's family.

Set a time and day for the service, preferably as soon as possible after the incident has taken place. If transportation will require the use of a bus or vans, make the necessary arrangements.

Notify your Mobile Church group, as well as the parish congregation at large, if possible. Invite the participation of all teens in your religious education program or school.

Notify the victim's family and, if possible, the friends of the victim, about the prayer service and give them as many details as you can.

After arriving at the site, follow a structure like the following:

- Introduce the group to the family and the family to the group.

- Summarize what happened at the site.

- Invite the family or friends to share memories of the victim.

- Invite spontaneous prayer or distribute copies of the prepared prayer service. If the prayer is spontaneous in nature, include prayers based on the memories that have just been shared.

- Sing an appropriate song, recite a meaningful poem, or have a significant reading.

- Show support for the family and friends of the victim with hugs, words of thanks for their sharing, offers of continued prayer, and so on.

- If it is appropriate and allowable, close the prayer service by spraying the image of a small angel on the pavement, using a stencil and spray paint. This symbolizes the continuing presence of the victim in the lives of the family and friends.

The prayer service should last approximately 15-20 minutes, depending on the number of memories shared.

A source in the medical examiner's or coroner's office is a great help in securing the necessary information regarding the victim and his/her relatives.

In some areas, the prayer service should be celebrated during the daytime. This may hinder the presence of some high school students, but the safety factor must always reign supreme.

It is wise to let the victim's family decide if they want to notify the media. Some are opposed to having media attention, and others welcome the media. It should be left to the family to make the contacts if they choose.

Try to invite people from all denominations and religions. This should be a time to celebrate our unity as a human family—not a time of division due to belief.

Inform the public safety officials in your community that you are planning this project. Abide by any safety requests they make of the group.

Results

The prayer services are usually very successful. The families of the victims express appreciation. The Mobile Church group becomes more aware of the serious problems of others and how, very often, those problems and sorrows are the direct results of injustice and poverty. Curiosity usually causes passers-by to join in the service, which also helps increase public awareness of the needs of the community.

Reflection

Set limits and stay committed. Over time, people will come to expect a prayer service of this type for their own family or friends who are victims of crime or accident. Ask participants in the Mobile Church group to commit for one year, or some other reasonable time period.

As part of a church-based organization called "M.I.C.A.H.," I have been organizing prayer services and vigils for several years. They have been extremely successful. To date, the prayer services occur on a weekly basis and have been limited to homicide victims in the Milwaukee metropolitan area.

Depending on your community, it may be better to limit the prayer services to a particular type of crime or accident. It is also best if you can limit the number of prayer services to once a month. Obviously, the occurrences are unpredictable and you may need to be flexible, but to hold prayer services more frequently than once each month is often a greater commitment than many people can make. The number of participants may vary from service to service.

Sister Rose Stietz
St. Martin de Porres Catholic Church
Milwaukee, WI

Notes to the Leader

When everyone has gathered, distribute the prayer service you have prepared. (See sample on next page.) Begin with simple introductions to the family of the victim. The following is a suggested format:

We gather today to remember [N] *who was a victim of* [mention the incident that took the victim's life] *at this location on* [date].

Introduce yourself. If a small group is in attendance, each person may want to introduce himself or herself to the family. If a large group is present, you may wish to say:

We are the members and friends of the parish community of [name of parish].

Invite the family and friends of the victim to introduce themselves, and if they wish, to share a memory about the person for whom you are gathered to pray.

Conclude the introductions and introduce the prayer service by saying:

And so, it is with [N] *in mind that we pray.*

The Mobile Church

Leader Blessed are You, Lord our God, keeper of the Book of Life.

All God of gentle mercy, remember [N]. Remember family and friends who are in sorrow at this time. Support them with your Holy Spirit and grant them the courage to accept this part of your plan of life.

Leader Blessed are You, Lord our God, keeper of the Book of Life.

Reader *1 Thessalonians 4:13-14, 16-17*
But we do not want you to be uninformed, brothers and sisters, about those who have died, so that you may not grieve as others do who have no hope. For since we believe that Jesus died and rose again, even so, through Jesus, God will bring with him those who have died.... For the Lord himself, with a cry of command, with the archangel's call and with the sound of God's trumpet, will descend from heaven, and the dead in Christ will rise first. Then we who are alive, who are left, will be caught up in the clouds together with them to meet the Lord in the air; and so we will be with the Lord forever.

Leader God, grant [N] eternal rest.

All God of gentle mercy, hear our prayer.

Leader God, grant consolation to those who grieve the loss of [N].

All God of gentle mercy, hear our prayer.

Leader God, grant that we may remember with joy the good brought into our lives through [N].

All God of gentle mercy, hear our prayer.

Leader God, grant us all strength and perseverance during this time of great sorrow.

All God of gentle mercy, hear our prayer.

Leader God of gentle mercy, we celebrate the entrance of [N] into eternal life. Your Son promised resurrection and happiness to all who follow him. We pray that with [N] we may come to share the everlasting fullness of heaven. We ask this through Jesus the Christ.

All Amen.

Parents' Day Out

Purpose of Project

Give parents a day of free time to shop, wrap gifts, make other holiday preparations—or take a break from holiday preparations.

Scripture References

Galatians 3:26-28

In Christ Jesus you are all children of God through faith. As many of you as were baptized into Christ have clothed yourselves with Christ. There is no longer Jew or Greek, there is no longer slave or free, there is no longer male and female; for all of you are one in Christ Jesus.

Catholic Social Teachings

Communities of Salt and Light [2] U.S. Bishops, 1993

In urban neighborhoods, in suburban communities, and in rural areas, parishes serve as anchors of hope and communities of caring, help families meet their own needs and reach out to others, and serve as centers of community life and networks of assistance.

Communities Involved

Youth of the parish, parents with younger children, and the younger children themselves. The wider community is also served through the collection of hats, mittens, and scarves to be given to the Salvation Army. This is the only "fee" asked of the parents.

Project Time Line

Set the Parents' Day Out for a Saturday in early December. About a month before, meet with youth and adult leaders to prepare a flyer and bulletin announcement, plan activities, and decide on the lunch menu. (See sample announcement on page 45.) The planning takes from three to five hours and includes shopping for supplies, as well as getting some of the craft projects ready for the younger children.

Project Description

Begin the day at 9:00 a.m. with the youth. Organize the materials and the spaces for the craft activities, lunch, video entertainment, and prayer time. Have the children arrive at 11:00 a.m. Collect mittens, scarves, and hats in a basket or decorated box. The parents should pick up the children about 3:45 p.m., or time the parents' arrival so that they can easily go to your parish's Saturday evening Mass if they wish.

Special Considerations

Divide the children into two groups, ages 3-6 and 7-11, so that crafts and videos can be geared toward the appropriate age level. Having two large gathering spaces is an advantage for this project, but not absolutely necessary.

Conduct a call-in registration if there is a concern about the numbers of children who may participate.

Results

Our typical experience is to have 30-35 young children with 10 teens.

Reflection

The parish community was enhanced by the relationships established by the youth and the young children. The contribution to the larger community becomes evident when the basket or box of hats, mittens, and scarves is placed next to the parish Giving Tree.

Remarks

Over the years this has been a heartwarming activity that is well worth the effort.

Parent quote, "I am delighted to have this opportunity for my children to have a fun day in a spiritually safe environment with other children from the parish."

Adapted from project by

Mary VanSchyndel
Coordinator of Religious Education
St. Joseph Parish
Oneida, WI

Andrea Sabor
Department of Total Catholic Education
Diocese of Green Bay

CALLING ALL KIDS

(AGES 3–11)

December 11
11:00 AM to 3:45 PM
St. Joseph Parish Commons

ST. JOE'S YOUTH GROUP
is providing a
PARENTS' DAY OUT

Parents can use this opportunity to freely go about their holiday preparations. Craft activities, lunch, video entertainment, and prayer time are planned for the children in our care! Adult supervisors will be present.

(We are accepting donations of hats, scarves, and mittens that can be placed in the basket under our parish Giving Tree. We are collecting these clothing items in response to an appeal by our community's Salvation Army. Thank you.)

Raising Political Awareness

Raise awareness of the Christian responsibility for good citizenship resulting in participation in the political process.

Scripture References

Mark 12:14-17

And they came and said to him, "Teacher, we know that you are sincere, and show deference to no one; for you do not regard people with partiality, but teach the way of God in accordance with truth. Is it lawful to pay taxes to the emperor, or not? Should we pay them, or should we not?" But knowing their hypocrisy, he said to them, "Why are you putting me to the test? Bring me a denarius and let me see it." And they brought one. Then he said to them, "Whose head is this, and whose title?" They answered, "The emperor's." Jesus said to them, "Give to the emperor the things that are the emperor's, and to God the things that are God's."

Matthew 17: 24-27

When they reached Capernaum, the collectors of the temple tax came to Peter and said, "Does your teacher not pay the temple tax?" He said, "Yes, he does." And when he came home, Jesus spoke of it first, asking, "What do you think, Simon? From whom do kings of the earth take toll or tribute? From their children or from others?" When Peter said, "From others," Jesus said to him, "Then the children are free. However, so that we do not give offense to them, go to the sea and cast a hook; take the first fish that comes up; and when you open its mouth, you will find a coin; take that and give it to them for you and me."

Catholic Social Teachings

Political Responsibility [9-10]
U.S. Bishops, 1995

In today's world, concern for human life, social justice, and peace necessarily requires persons and organizations to participate in the political process in accordance with their own responsibilities and roles...As citizens, we are all called to become informed, active, and responsible participants in the political process. It is the laity who are primarily responsible for activity in political affairs.

A Call to Action [46]
(Octogesima Adveniens)
Pope Paul VI, 1971

To take politics seriously at its different levels—local, regional, national and worldwide—is to affirm the duty of [every man and woman] to recognize the concrete reality and the value of the freedom of choice that is offered to [them] to seek to bring about both the good of the city and of the nation and of [humanity]. Politics are a demanding manner—but not the only one—of living the Christian commitment to the service of others.

Communities Involved

Young people in grades 6-12 and the legislative bodies in your local or state community.

Project Timeline

Depending on the length of your sessions, this project can be done in one session or in two to three sessions. Various materials will be needed: 3 x 5 index cards, markers, tape, newsprint or poster board, current newspapers and periodicals, a Bible, the *Catechism of the Catholic Church,* and other social justice documents as you desire.

Project Description

Icebreaker—Who Am I?
Political Players Activity

Before the session, create a political name card for each young person in the group. Using a marker, write the names of historical political players on 3 x 5 cards. Some suggested names are George Washington, Abraham Lincoln, John F. Kennedy, Franklin D. Roosevelt, Martin Luther King, Jr., Richard Nixon, Dorothy Day, Barbara Jordan, Bill Clinton, Cesar Chavez, Hillary Clinton, George Bush, Sandra Day O'Connor, and Jesse Jackson. Be prepared with at least one idea of how each named person affected the political process in his or her time in history. In particular, know something about the issues that will be discussed later in this session.

At the beginning of the session, tape a card onto the back of each young person without allowing the participant to see the card. Allow five minutes for the participants to walk around and ask questions of one another to try to identify whose name is on their card. No more than three questions can be asked of any one individual. After five minutes, allow everyone to look at their cards. As a group, discuss what significant contribution each historical person made or makes to the political process.

Identifying a Course of Action

Ask one of the participants to read the quote on page 46 from the U.S. Bishops document, *Political Responsibility: Proclaiming the Gospel of Life, Protecting the Least Among Us, and Pursuing the Common Good.*

Discussion

Discuss these or similar questions:

- What does this statement mean or say to you?

- Do you agree with the statement concerning the responsibility of Catholic Christians within the political process?

- In what ways can you participate at your age now?

- In what ways can you participate when you become an adult?

Divide the large group into smaller groups of three or four. Instruct each group to elect a spokesperson and a recording secretary. Give each group the local (or state) and national sections of a newspaper. Have the group members search the paper for stories that address political situations. Examples might include health care issues, substance abuse, AIDS, discrimination, racism, or the environment. After finding several stories, the group should decide on one issue to address.

The group should then examine and assemble everything they know about the issue, using various resources and life experiences. Resources that could be supplied to the groups include: a Bible, the *Catechism of the Catholic Church*, the *Political Responsibility* document from the USCC, Catholic periodicals, and the internet. Emphasize that personal experiences can also be examined, including newscasts that have been viewed by individuals, stories that have been heard, or personal encounters with the situation. Information should be compiled on newsprint or poster board.

After compiling all they know about the political issue, the group should then brainstorm a Christian response to the situation. An action or statement should be chosen and written at the bottom of the group's newsprint or poster.

Finish by distributing the names and addresses of local or state government representatives. Each group, using the action or statement at the bottom of its newsprint, should draft a letter to one representative stating the following:

- the issue that the group has researched
- the Catholic Christian response to the issue
- the action the representative should take

Special Considerations

A list of local or state governmental officials must be secured from either the local newspaper or county government office.

Results

Young people sometimes feel helpless in the face of difficult political situations. This activity will give them a vehicle for researching a political issue and responding in a Catholic Christian manner by raising their voices to political figures.

Remarks

The icebreaker works best with younger adolescents. Also, consider asking the young people to type their letters to the governmental representatives.

Idea contributed by

John Dols, High School Religion Teacher
Xavier High School
Appleton, WI

Reach Across Boundaries

Purpose of Project

Promote acceptance of and appreciation for individuals with developmental disabilities.

Scripture References

1 Peter 4:10

Like good stewards of the manifold grace of God, serve one another with whatever gift each of you has received.

Matthew 11:4-5

Jesus answered them, "Go and tell John what you hear and see: the blind receive their sight, the lame walk, the lepers are cleansed, the deaf hear, the dead are raised, and the poor have good news brought to them."

Catholic Social Teachings

Pastoral Statement of U.S. Catholic Bishops on People with Disabilities [1, 9]
1978, Rev 1989

We call upon people of good will to reexamine their attitudes toward their disabled brothers and sisters and promote their well-being, acting with the sense of justice and the compassion that the Lord so clearly desires. Further, realizing the unique gifts disabled individuals have to offer the Church, we wish to address the need for their integration into the Christian community and their fuller participation in its life....

There can be no separate Church for persons with disabilities. We are one flock that follows a single shepherd.

Communities Involved

Young people in grades 6-12 and residents of a group home or other residential facility for persons with developmental disabilities.

Project Time Line

This is always a popular activity during the Christmas season, but it works well in other seasons also, such as St. Valentine's Day.

After scheduling an evening that works for both the staff of the group home and for your own group, promote the activity by advertising it in the parish bulletin for several weeks before the event.

The celebration should last about one hour. This works best for the home since it can be easily scheduled between residents' dinner hour and bed time.

Create an informational sheet about the event. Decorate it with clip art and either incorporate a permission form with the information sheet or attach one to it. (See sample forms on pages 54 and 55.) Make it available at the school, and for the youth ministry, or religious education program for grades 6-12. Plan to have participants meet at the church or school and travel together to the home. For this reason, it is necessary to have an accurate count of participants at least one day before the project in order to ensure enough drivers.

If the celebration will be during Christmastime, prepare a small booklet of familiar Christmas songs. Stick with the basics. For example, "Jingle Bells," "Frosty the Snowman," and "Silent Night" are always popular. If at all possible, arrange for someone to play the guitar for accompaniment. Bring along a tambourine and jingle bells, too.

Gather supplies you will need for your activity and always have small prizes to distribute.

Prepare the Christmas Bingo game as follows:

1. Make the Playing Cards

Since each Bingo playing card must be unique, the creation of the Bingo cards can be time consuming. Start by making a master grid of 25 squares (1¾" each) on a piece of 8 ½" by 11" paper. Find 25 seasonal pictures (star, tree, angel, trumpet, snowman, etc.) and reduce each picture on a copier so it will fit into a square in the master grid.

Using either tape or removable glue, place a piece of clip art in each of the 25 squares. Make a photocopy of the completed grid and use this as your first playing card.

Now, lift the clip art carefully from the master grid and rearrange it to make a different pattern for your second playing card.

Repeat the process of rearranging the clip art and making one copy of each arrangement until you have as many playing cards as you need. Using colored paper adds to the festiveness of the cards.

2. Make the Calling Cards

For your calling cards, enlarge each piece of clip art to 8½" by 11" and glue each one to a piece of construction paper. You can write the name of the card on its back for the caller's benefit. As each card is called, the caller should hold up the enlargement so that all can see it. Many residents have poor eye sight, and it is helpful to see an enlarged version of the image they are looking for.

After creating your game, save it to use again.

The Event: *Introductions and Welcome*	Begin the time together by having each participant introduce himself or herself to the residents. Expect a warm welcome that could include smiles, handshakes, and hugs.
Singing	After introductions and a short visiting time, distribute the song books. Even if you have no accompanist, the residents of the group home usually enjoy shaking tambourines and bells.
Christmas Bingo	During the activity, each youth participant should find a buddy or two to help during the game. Consider using wrapped candy for Bingo markers. Chocolate kisses and wrapped peppermints work well.
Prizes	Prizes are always welcomed with many smiles! Be sure to have a variety of prizes in case someone wins more than once. And also make sure that everyone gets at least one prize, whether they win the game or not. Christmas cookies, candy, pretzels or other snacks packaged in small bags and tied with bright ribbon are good prizes that the staff of the home can monitor for each resident. A popular substitute for shouting "Bingo" is to say "Ho, Ho, Ho!" in celebration of the season.
Departing	Often, saying good-bye can be difficult, especially since the young people have had such a fun time together with the residents! If you repeat this activity for other occasions (Valentine's Day, St. Patrick's Day, Easter, etc.,) you will be able to tell the residents that your group will see them again soon.

Special Considerations

There must be a group home or residential facility for people with developmental disabilities nearby, although the idea could be adjusted for use in a nursing home setting. There must also be a sufficient number of chaperones and drivers for the number of youth attending. Be sure to become familiar with the setting in which you will be spending time. Group homes are designed to be like any other home, so rooms will most likely not accommodate more than fifteen people or so.

Results

The youth share their time, their intellect, and their voices. They have a one-on-one experience in which they learn that persons with developmental disabilities need not be feared, but that they are special creations of God. The residents of the group home share their joy and wonder at our presence and the celebration of the season. Everyone shares in a celebration of life!

Reflection

Youth who have participated in this activity have come away with a positive experience and a desire to repeat the project soon. They have experienced an awakened sense of the miracle of their own lives and the dignity of all life.

Remarks

Season-appropriate songs are always appreciated, but if you need extras, we've found that Christmas carols are fun and popular year-round!

Submitted by

Anna Vosters & Peg VandeHey
Coordinators of Youth Ministry
St. Thomas More Parish
Appleton, WI

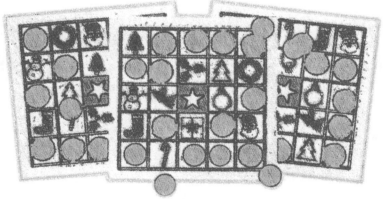

YOU'RE INVITED!!!

St. Thomas More's
Agape Home Christmas Party

Come along and visit with Agape Home residents as we

⭐ **Play Christmas Bingo**

⭐ **Sing Christmas Carols**

⭐ **Laugh and Celebrate God's love for each of us . . .**
no matter what our disability or struggle may be!

When?   **We're leaving the STM parking lot at**
6:00 p.m., Tues, Dec. 19.
(Gather in the Youth Room before leaving.)
We'll return to STM around 8:00 p.m.

Remember...   • **to complete & return the Release Form.**
                • **to let us know by Monday, Dec. 18 if**
                  you plan on joining us. (We need to
                  arrange enough drivers.)

Lots of *SMILES, LAUGHTER,*
and *JOYFUL VOICES*
are guaranteed.
Don't miss the fun!

Reach Across Boundaries

RELEASE

In consideration of [parish/school name] arranging for a trip to [destination] on [date and time], I , the undersigned parent of _____ in grade _____, a minor, hereby releases and agrees to hold harmless the above named parish and/or any of its advisors, chaperones or persons connected with this event, from any liability, claims, damages for personal injury, property loss, or other damage which may result during the above event.

The undersigned student hereby agrees to abide by the rules established for the above event.

Dated at _____ [city and state], this _____ day of _____ [month], _____ [year].

𝒙_____   **𝒙**_____
Signature of Parent or Guardian   Signature of Participant

Please complete the following:

_____   _____   _____
Child's Name   Birth Date   Home Phone

_____   _____
Address   City / State / Zip Code

_____   _____   _____
Father's Name   Place of Employment   Work Phone

_____   _____   _____
Mother's Name   Place of Employment   Work Phone

_____   _____
Child's Physician   Office Phone

_____   _____
Family Physician   Office Phone

_____   _____
Insurance Company   Policy Number

AUTHORIZATION FOR MEDICAL TREATMENT

I hereby authorize the treatment, administration of anesthesia and/or surgical treatment(s) for my minor son/daughter _____ in the event of a medical situation occurring during my absence or when the hospital or physician(s) are unable to contact me. This authorization extends to any hospital, physician(s), and nursing personnel within the physician's staff where treatment is rendered in the physician's office. I release from medical responsibility and liability the hospital, physician(s), and nursing personnel for performing medical procedures acting on the authority of this medical treatment consent form which such medical providers deem necessary for my minor child.

Signed this _____ day of _____, _____ and valid through _____[date].

Parent Signature **𝒙**_____

Please use the back of this page to list any special medical conditions or other necessary health information.

Send Your Clothes South for the Winter

Purpose of Project

This activity helps to connect the young people to the broader Church and its needs. The parish heard of a need for clothes in Mississippi and connected with another parish to accomplish this clothes drive. The store in Mississippi was chosen because it did not give away the clothes but, rather, sold the clothes at a reduced cost to those in need. This preserves the dignity of the working poor. The parish in the North collected the clothes during November and shipped the clothes South during Advent, in time for Christmas.

Scripture References

Acts 2:42-45

They devoted themselves to the apostles' teaching and fellowship, to the breaking of bread and the prayers. Awe came upon everyone, because many wonders and signs were being done by the apostles. All who believed were together and had all things in common; they would sell their possessions and goods and distribute the proceeds to all, as any had need.

Catholic Social Teachings

Pastoral Constitution on the Church in the Modern World [26] *(Gaudium et Spes)* Vatican Council II, 1965

Every social group must take account of the needs and aspirations of other groups and even of the general welfare of the entire human family.

Peace on Earth [11] *(Pacem et Terris)* Pope John XXIII, 1963

[Everyone] has the right to life, to bodily integrity, and to the means which are suitable for the proper development of life; these are primarily food, clothing, shelter, rest, medical care, and finally the necessary social services.

Economic Justice for All [86] U.S. Bishops, 1986

The obligation to provide justice for all means that the poor have the single most urgent economic claim on the conscience of the nation.

Communities Involved

Young people from the parish plan and organize the activity. They also participate, along with adults. Recipients are customers of a thrift store or other organization that assists the poor. In some cases, sponsors include businesses, parish groups, or service organizations.

Project Time Line

In early October, determine the thrift store, organization, or agency with whom you will work. Set the clothing collection for the four weekends of November. Invite the whole parish to participate in the sorting and packing session held on the evening of the first Sunday of Advent.

Project Description

In a religious education session, youth ministry activity, or school religion class, discuss the importance of Christian service in Catholic Christian living. Share the story of the people who are customers of the thrift store or clients of another service organization. Speak about the plight of the children whose parents will purchase the clothes. Invite the youth to share their stories about serving in the community and how it has affected others and themselves.

Form a committee of youth who want to work on the project. Divide the group into sub-committees to work on publicity, collection, sorting, packing, and delivering. If delivery will require shipping, be sure to have those arrangements made in advance of the packing party. Try to work closely with the other staff in the parish so that the entire parish is invited to participate. Ideally, the clothes collection is mentioned by the celebrant and/or included in the petitions at each Sunday Mass during the drive.

Select an area in the parish building to store the boxes of clothing as they are filled. Having all or part of the stockpile in the back of the church forces people to walk around the clothes, which acts as a reminder not only of the project and the people who will be helped but also of one's personal wealth and the need to be generous with what one owns.

At the end of the clothing drive, have a packaging party in which young people and parishioners sort the clothes according to type and size (children's shoes in one set of boxes, men's shoes in another). Adequately secure the boxes for shipping.

If you are not familiar with a local thrift store, or know of an agency or group out of your area with whom you can work, your St. Vincent de Paul groups or the Salvation Army are good places to begin your search.

Large boxes are needed. A good contact is a local trucking company or a moving and storage center. You can often get either donated boxes or a discounted price on them.

Shipping costs can be covered either through a special collection or fund-raiser or, if possible, out of the parish budget. The ideal is to arrange a sponsorship with a trucking company who would provide the shipping free.

Results

This is a good intergenerational activity that allows the teens to be the leaders. The entire parish is involved but the young people are really the initiators and the ones who direct the project. The clothing collection activity helped the youth see the needs of the poor and realize that they can make a difference.

Reflection

Our clothing drive was the project of our Confirmation candidates. They were very proud of themselves and amazed that they could lead an intergenerational parish activity. The response from the parish exceeded the goal of the planning group. The students were able to create an excitement for this project because of their passion to serve others. The project helped them truly to see a need and address it in meaningful ways, which created an ongoing desire in a number of them to continue participating in community service. This project connected people in the parish who would not have met otherwise, and sparked an awareness of God's call for all of us to be of service to others, especially those in need.

Remarks

Our parish chose a thrift store in Hernando, Mississippi, as its target recipient. Sacred Heart Southern Mission in Mississippi was the sponsoring agency.

Submitted by

Sandy Mangin
Campus Minister
St. Mary's Central High School
Menash, WI

Ellen Mommaerts
Youth Minister
St. Agnes Parish
Green Bay, WI

"...whoever wishes to become great among you

must be your servant...."
Mark 10:43

Service Mapping

Purpose of Project

Raise awareness of young people and parish families about the opportunities for service in the parish and local community. Encourage service to others in both the parish and civic communities.

Scripture References

Mark 10:41-45

When the ten heard this, they began to be angry with James and John. So Jesus called them and said to them, "You know that among the Gentiles those whom they recognize as their rulers lord it over them, and their great ones are tyrants over them. But it is not so among you; but whoever wishes to become great among you must be your servant, and whoever wishes to be first among you must be slave of all. For the Son of Man came not to be served but to serve, and to give his life a ransom for many."

Catholic Social Teachings

Peace on Earth [146]
(Pacem in Terris)
Pope John XXIII, 1963

Once again we exhort our children to take an active part in public life, and to contribute towards the attainment of the common good of the entire human family as well as to that of their own country. They should endeavor, therefore, in the light of the Faith and with the strength of love, to ensure that the various institutions—whether economic, social, cultural or political in purpose—should be such as not to create obstacles, but rather to facilitate or render less arduous [humanity's] perfectioning of itself both in the natural order as well as in the supernatural.

Communities Involved

Young people in the parish. Civic and parish organizations.

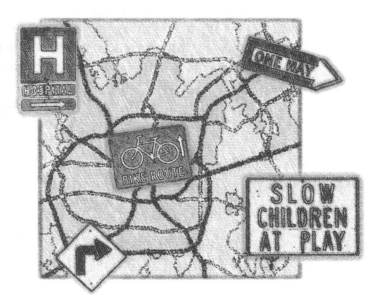

Project Time Line

In August, establish a committee of young people who are willing to take on monthly responsibilities of publishing a newsletter from September through July. The commitment to this project is for a one-year period.

Project Description

A team of news reporters publish a monthly Service Newsletter to raise awareness in the parish community about local needs and how they can be served.

The team's monthly responsibilities include:

- identify, contact, and write articles about three parish and/or civic service organizations (see sample Service Opportunities, page 64)
- interview and write a profile story about someone who is or has been involved in a service project in the community or parish (see sample Interview form, page 65)
- assemble a newsletter, featuring the profile story and the three articles about service opportunities in the area
- duplicate the correct number of newsletters and arrange with the parish to insert them in the parish bulletins

Special Considerations

It is important to establish a time commitment from the participants to this endeavor. A one-year commitment works well for a monthly publication. If your group cannot publish monthly, perhaps every other month would work better.

Results

The Service Opportunities and Interview guide sheets were very helpful in keeping "reporters" on track. A binder with copies of Service Opportunities was displayed along with the other parish literature in the back of church. Thirty-two opportunities were identified including the various parish ministries. Each month, the four pieces—the profile and the three service opportunities—were published in the parish bulletin, one each week. While that was not the original plan, it was cost-saving. This endeavor was briefly described in the bulletin the fourth week of August.

Reflection

The binder with the service opportunities became an excellent resource for those young people who were requested to do service projects in preparation for Confirmation.

Remarks

One adult volunteer was particularly pleased to see young people interested in service to others, i.e., "doing things for others without expecting anything in return." Most gratifying, however, was the young people's ability to identify and talk about the various opportunities in the parish and community. Service opportunities became a point of conversation! This information can become dated within a year or two. So if it is to be used for a period of time, a system for updating has to be incorporated.

Submitted by

Chris Broslavick
Department of Education
Diocese of Green Bay, WI

SERVICE OPPORTUNITIES

Organization _____

Primary focus of the organization's work _____

Contact person _____ Phone # _____

Service opportunity for young people…

Task(s) _____

Location _____

Time of year _____

Special considerations _____

Service opportunity for adults…

Task(s) _____

Location _____

Time of year _____

Special considerations _____

Service opportunity for families…

Task(s) _____

Location _____

Time of year _____

Special considerations _____

Note to Reporters: When featuring a "Service Champion" for the Newsletter, please use the following "Interview Starters" to gather information for your story. Be alert to capturing good direct quotes.

INTERVIEW STARTERS...

Name _____

Organization or service activity _____

_____

What do you do? _____

How often? _____ Where? _____

How did you become involved? _____

_____

How long have you been involved? _____

Why are you committed to this service activity? _____

_____

How is your work helping others? _____

_____

How is your service affecting your faith life, your attitudes? _____

_____

How do your family and friends view your commitment to this activity? _____

_____

What would you say to young people about service to others? _____

_____

Service Night

Purpose of Project

Allow youths in grades 6-11 to engage in various community service events on the same evening.

Scripture References

Matthew 19:16-22

Then someone came to him and said, "Teacher, what good deed must I do to have eternal life?" And he said to him, "Why do you ask me about what is good? There is only one who is good. If you wish to enter into life, keep the commandments." He said to him, "Which ones?" And Jesus said, "You shall not murder; You shall not commit adultery; You shall not steal; You shall not bear false witness; Honor your father and mother; also, You shall love your neighbor as yourself." The young man said to him, "I have kept all these; what do I still lack?" Jesus said to him, "If you wish to be perfect, go, sell your possessions, and give the money to the poor, and you will have treasure in heaven; then come, follow me." When the young man heard this word, he went away grieving, for he had many possessions.

Matthew 25:14-16

[Jesus said] "For it is as if a man, going on a journey, summoned his slaves and entrusted his property to them; to one he gave five talents, to another two, to another one, to each according to his ability. Then he went away. The one who had received the five talents went off at once and traded with them, and made five more talents."

Catholic Social Teachings

The Hundredth Year [11]
(Centesimus Annus)
Pope John Paul II, 1991

The human being "is the only creature on earth which God willed for itself"... conferring [upon human beings] an incomparable dignity. In effect, beyond the rights which one acquires by one's own work, there exist rights which do not correspond to any work performed, but which flow from one's essential dignity as a person.

Communities Involved

Parish youth, catechists and/or youth minister, parents, as well as the various groups that are part of the service projects selected, e.g., senior citizens, nursing home residents, day-care participants, a parish food pantry, residents of a home for young unmarried mothers.

Project Time Line

Approximately three sessions over a period of two months are needed to plan and conduct a Service Night. The actual event is from 5:45 - 8:15 p.m. on the night of the project.

Prior to Session 1

Session 1

A Baker's-Dozen of Service Ideas

Compile a list of service opportunities (see suggestions below).

Students and leaders gather and consult your list of service opportunities. Here are a few suggestions:

1. Hold a baby shower or children's birthday party to collect items for needy infants and children. Invite recipients as guests of honor.

2. Collect food to give to the needy within the community. Have a scavenger hunt for food in a neighborhood to collect certain items on a prepared list—divide into teams and have an adult driver with a large car or truck. Offer a prize for the first team to obtain everything on its list.

3. Serve at a local hospital or other care center: prepare baskets or decorated bags that contain toiletries as well as flowers or fruit, a general interest magazine or novel, and supportive and encouraging personal notes.

4. Engage in service to the homebound by providing for their spiritual needs: write prayer cards, collect religious articles to be distributed, make an audio or video tape of Sunday Mass, make an audio tape of yourself reading from a spiritual book or the Bible, mail parish bulletins to shut-ins, deliver palms, an Easter basket, or a potted and decorated Christmas tree (as is seasonally appropriate).

5. Plan a party or dance for senior citizens.

6. Write to government representatives or others in authority about supporting the interests of the poor.

7. Prepare baked goods or a meal to share with a homeless shelter or another group.

8. Have a movie or game night and charge admission of paper products, household items, or usable clothing to give to the needy.

9. Work to improve literacy in your local community: collect good, used reading material, such as recent magazines, unused puzzle books, and fiction and nonfiction books. Read to children at a local library or after-school program.

10. Make a quilt (with symbols and messages of hope) for the ill, homebound, or frail elderly.

11. Entertain children in homeless shelters or children with disabilities by taking them to the movies, a sports event, zoo, or museum.

12. Perform skits of Bible stories or lives of the saints for the younger children in the parish.

13. Prepare bag lunches or assemble bags with shower or bathing needs for the homeless.

Session 2

Distribute information sheets and consent forms so that the parents and guardians will be informed of the plans for the Service Night. An adult organizer should make arrangements with the various sites that will be involved and for any transportation needs.

Session 3

As the youth and chaperones assemble, collect the permission slips, give any last minute instructions, and pray with the group before the individuals depart for their events.

Special Considerations

Transportation—Adhere to all local policies regarding transportation. Bus transportation is ideal for large groups.

Expenses—Anticipate and arrange for any expenses. Contingency funds should be available so that all those who are interested are able to participate.

Parent participation—Invite parents to become involved in helping with arrangements, chaperoning, and other details.

Results

Young people were able to visit six different sites in one evening. The event went very smoothly because the pre-planning was so comprehensive (contacts made, travel routes planned, materials prepared). An increasing number of students and parents are participating each year. They seem to look forward to working together.

Reflection

Service Night gives witness to the message to share time, talent, and treasure with others less fortunate than we are. It is the way we live out the corporal works of mercy, putting faith into practice.

For future Service Nights, we plan to have a culminating prayer service that evening, which will allow each group to briefly share their experiences.

Remarks

This project provides opportunities for both youth and leaders to give input and make a contribution. Parents have expressed their appreciation of the structure and organization of the event.

Adapted from project by

Andrea Sabor
Department of Total Catholic Education
Diocese of Green Bay

The Shirt Off Your Back

Purpose of Project

To invite young people to share tee shirts or sweatshirts from their personal wardrobes with those who need clothing.

Scripture References

Luke 3:10-11

And the crowds asked him, "What then should we do?" In reply he said to them, "Whoever has two coats must share with anyone who has none; and whoever has food must do likewise."

Matthew 25:38, 40

"And when was it that we saw you a stranger and welcomed you, or naked and gave you clothing?" And the king will answer them, "Truly I tell you, just as you did it to one of the least of these who are members of my family, you did it to me."

Catholic Social Teachings

A Call to Action [23]
(Octogesima Adveniens)
Pope Paul VI, 1971

In teaching us charity, the Gospel instructs us in the preferential respect due to the poor and the special situation they have in society: the more fortunate should renounce some of their rights so as to place their goods more generously at the service of others.

Economic Justice for All [16]
U.S. Bishops, 1986

As followers of Christ, we are challenged to make a fundamental "option for the poor"—to speak for the voiceless, to defend the defenseless, to assess life-styles, policies, and social institutions in terms of their impact on the poor. This "option for the poor" does not mean pitting one group against another, but rather, strengthening the whole community by assisting those who are most vulnerable. As Christians, we are called to respond to the needs of *all* our brothers and sisters, but those with the greatest needs require the greatest response.

Communities Involved

Young people in the parish school, religious education program, or youth ministry program. People served by the organizations who receive the clothing, such as a thrift shop, Salvation Army, St. Vincent de Paul Society, or needy parish.

Project Time Line

Two sessions are required to complete this project, one is an informative session and the other for the collection itself. The Thanksgiving season is always a nice time for this project, but it needn't be limited to one season.

Project Description

Prior to the first session, these tasks should be accomplished:

1. Recruit a laundry or dry cleaner to clean the shirts. If possible, arrange for the establishment to donate their services or to offer them at a significantly reduced rate. If there is a fee involved, the money will need to be raised through a fund-raising activity. You might also invite some of the young people to launder the shirts at their homes.

2. Invite a person from the participating organization (thrift shop, Salvation Army, St. Vincent de Paul Society, parish) to talk to the young people.

3. Collect large boxes from a local shipper or manufacturing company.

4. Arrange with one of the young people to prepare to explain the details of the project to the rest of the group.

Optional: Make posters to promote the event.

Session One

The representative from the participating organization speaks to the group, explaining the work they do and giving some insight into the needs of the people they serve.

At the end of the presentation, the prepared young person explains the specific details of the tee shirt and sweatshirt collection, including the date, time and place. The students should be invited to wear two tee shirts or a sweatshirt over a tee shirt on the day of the collection. At some point in the program, the young people will be invited to take off one of the tee shirts or the sweatshirt and place it in the collection box.

Session Two

On the day of the collection, either in the context of class, a youth gathering, or liturgy, invite the young people to take off one of their shirts and place it in one of the boxes. A short presentation of thanks should be given either by one of the group or by a representative from the participating organization.

Following the collection, bring the shirts to the predetermined dry cleaners to have the shirts cleaned and packaged. Then see to their delivery to the organization.

Special Considerations

If this activity does not take place during a liturgy, it is always a good idea to prepare a short prayer service with the theme of caring for the needs of the poor. Incorporate the collection of the shirts into the service.

Results

The school collected more than 500 tee shirts and sweatshirts that were sent to an inner city parish in Chicago. The shirts were presented to the gospel choir from the parish when they came to perform at the school.

Reflection

This was a wonderful way to visually express the scripture passage that states if we have two coats, we should give one to the poor. In this case, shirts were the commodity that was shared, and the young people who received them were truly grateful.

Remarks

Weeks after the collection, shirts continued to be collected by the school. These "late arrivals" were delivered by students from the school who were doing service in the inner city of Chicago.

Idea contributed by

Jane Hall
Campus Minister
Notre Dame de la Baie Academy
Green Bay, WI

Social Concerns

Purpose of Project

Provide a practical process to help older adolescents reflect on current social problems in light of the Gospel and discuss what the Christian response should be. Encourage the group to agree upon a specific issue in the world, learn about it, reflect upon it, and respond to it as Church.

Scripture References

Matthew 5:13-16

"You are the salt of the earth; but if salt has lost its taste, how can its saltiness be restored? It is no longer good for anything, but is thrown out and trampled under foot.

"You are the light of the world. A city built on a hill cannot be hid. No one after lighting a lamp puts it under the bushel basket, but on the lampstand, and it gives light to all in the house. In the same way, let your light shine before others, so that they may see your good works and give glory to your Father in heaven."

Matthew 14:15-21

When it was evening, the disciples came to him and said, "This is a deserted place, and the hour is now late; send the crowds away so that they may go into the villages and buy food for themselves." Jesus said to them, "They need not go away; you give them something to eat." They replied, "We have nothing here but five loaves and two fish."And he said, "Bring them here to me." Then he ordered the crowds to sit down on the grass. Taking the five loaves and the two fish, he looked up to heaven, and blessed and broke the loaves, and gave them to the disciples, and the disciples gave them to the crowds. And all ate and were filled; and they took up what was left over of the broken pieces, twelve baskets full. And those who ate were about five thousand men, besides women and children.

1 John 3:17

How does God's love abide in anyone who has the world's goods and sees a brother or sister in need and yet refuses help?

Isaiah 61:1-2

The spirit of the Lord God is upon me, because the Lord has anointed me; he has sent me to bring good news to the oppressed, to bind up the brokenhearted, to proclaim liberty to the captives, and release to the prisoners; to proclaim the year of the Lord's favor, and the day of vengeance of our God; to comfort all who mourn.

Catholic Social Teachings

Pastoral Constitution on the Church in the Modern World [69] *(Gaudiem et Spes)* Vatican Council II, 1965

The right to have a share of earthly goods sufficient for oneself and one's family belongs to everyone. The Fathers and Doctors of the church held this view, teaching that [all] are obliged to come to the relief of the poor, and to do so not merely out of their superfluous goods.

The Hundredth Year [58]
(Centessimus Annus)
Pope John Paul II, 1991

Love for others, and in the first place love for the poor, in whom the Church sees Christ himself, is made concrete in the promotion of justice. Justice will never be fully attained unless people see in the poor person, who is asking for help in order to survive, not an annoyance or a burden, but an opportunity for showing kindness and a chance for greater enrichment. Only such an awareness can give the courage needed to face the risk and the change involved in every authentic attempt to come to the aid of another.

Communities Involved

High school juniors and seniors

Project Time Line

Because of the number of steps involved in this process, several sessions or meetings should be devoted to preparing for the projects. The overall time line, in addition to the preparation process, is dependent on the projects that the young people choose and the commitment they make to them.

Project Description

In order to help identify areas of need and to discern which of these areas to work in, lead the group through the following activities. You will need to divide them according to your particular time frame.

- *Journaling Activity*—Invite participants to respond to the question: What do you believe to be the three most important messages of the Christian scriptures that are either spoken or modeled by Jesus or his followers?

- *Scripture Search*—Divide the young people into small groups and assign each group several scripture passages from the following list. Each group should specifically, but briefly, name the qualities of service, justice, or discipleship found in the passages.

Matthew 4:18-22	Luke 5:29-32
Matthew 5:1-16	Luke 10:29-37
Matthew 6:1-4	Luke 12:13-21
Matthew 9:10-13	Luke 16:19-31
Matthew 10:1-15	Luke 19:1-10
Matthew 19:16-22	John 11:1-45
Matthew 25:31-46	John 13:1-20
Mark 12:41-44	John 21:15-19

- *If the Scriptures Were Written Today*—With a young person at the chalkboard, ask the participants to respond to the question: "If Jesus of Nazareth walked the earth today, whom do you think he would seek out with the same compassion and tenderness that he did 2,000 years ago?" Have them give specific names or groups of people in their answers. The young person at the board should record the responses. Once they have listed their suggestions, ask them to negotiate and come to a decision on the group's top two choices for whom Jesus would model the perfect idea of love and service.

- *In Teens' Eyes*—Pose the following challenge to the group: Jesus has just sent a message that in one hour he will come to anyone or any group of people that we want. Where should we send Jesus?

- *The Catholic Community's Role*—Ask the group to briefly discuss the following:

  What role does the Church play in serving the needy in today's world?

  What is the difference between a person working on his or her own for a better world and the Church community working together?

  Read and discuss the two quotes from *Catholic Social Teachings* on pages 73 and 74.

- *Jesus Called*—Advise the young people that Jesus called and he has an emergency. He will not be able to visit the group's first choice that was determined in the activity *If the Scriptures Were Written Today.* Jesus invites his Church (this group) to go in his name. They must be a sign of his love and compassion in the world.

- *Where to Go?*—The young people come to a consensus whether to serve their first choice or not.

- *Becoming Informed*—Either by personal study or by inviting a witness speaker to address the group, learn more about the specific issue or charity the group has selected.

- *Getting Organized*—The young people should select the way or type of outreach that they will pursue to respond to the Lord's challenge. They should choose the date, time, site, transportation, and materials needed for the service. They might also divide into task-related groups according to interest, skills and gifts.

- *Solicitation of Donations*—If monies are needed to fund this outreach, a strategy for fund-raising should be developed. This might become the responsibility of one of the task-related groups mentioned above.

- *Make the Event Come to Life*—Implement the plan that has been developed using this process.

- *Group Process*—In a prayerful, group setting, reflect upon the experience in light of their understanding of scripture, Catholic Social Teachings, and their personal observations from the experience. Ask the following evaluative questions and record the responses:

  What was successful about this service event?

  What could be improved about this service event?

- *Offering Praise to God*—Gather in a circle. Ask the young people to offer thanks to God in a spontaneous manner. Close with the Lord's Prayer.

Special Considerations

This project assumes that the young people have reached a level of faith maturity that allows for a discussion of discipleship, service, the role and responsibilities of those baptized and confirmed, and issues of justice and morality. It is best reserved for juniors and seniors in high school. This is a good process to include as a segment in a high school Confirmation program.

Results

The young people were delighted in being able to work together as well as being allowed to explore their own interests when combining this process of group service with individual service opportunities. In one parish, the confirmands chose service opportunities at the following sites: a homeless shelter, food pantry, Big Brothers/Big Sisters organization, a children's hospital, and the Ronald McDonald House.

Reflection

The young people are moved to an adult faith and understanding by their own ownership of their faith. There is a connection made between faith, community, and service.

Adapted from project by

Mary Ann Jasiak
Director of Religious Education
Holy Name Parish
Kimberly, WI

Stock Sale

Purpose of Project

Raise funds for a service opportunity or cause, while also increasing awareness throughout the parish of the needs of the people who are served through the project.

Scripture References

Mark 12:41-44

He sat down opposite the treasury, and watched the crowd putting money into the treasury. Many rich people put in large sums. A poor widow came and put in two small copper coins, which are worth a penny. Then he called his disciples and said to them, "Truly I tell you, this poor widow has put in more than all those who are contributing to the treasury. For all of them have contributed out of their abundance; but she out of her poverty has put in everything she had, all she had to live on."

Matthew 19:21

[Jesus said] "If you wish to be perfect, go, sell your possessions, and give the money to the poor, and you will have treasure in heaven; then come, follow me."

Catholic Social Teachings

Pastoral Constitution on the Church in the Modern World [30] *(Gaudium et Spes)* Vatican Council II, 1965

Profound and rapid changes make it particularly urgent that no one [be content] with a merely individualistic morality. It grows increasingly true that the obligations of justice and love are fulfilled only if each person…promotes and assists the public and private institutions dedicated to bettering the conditions of human life.

A Call to Action [23] *(Octogesima Adveniens)* Pope Paul VI, 1971

In teaching us charity, the Gospel instructs us in the preferential respect due to the poor and the special situation they have in society: the more fortunate should renounce some of their rights so as to place their goods more generously at the service of others.

Economic Justice for All [17] U.S. Bishops, 1986

Human rights are the minimum conditions for life in community. In Catholic teaching, human rights include not only civil and political rights but also economic rights….This means that when people are without a chance to earn a living, and must go hungry and homeless, they are being denied basic rights. Society must ensure that these rights are protected.

Communities Involved

High school teens and their families, friends, and acquaintances, as well as the rest of the parish community.

Project Time Line

The Stock Sale is a three-month process of choosing, publicizing, and following up on whatever project you pursue.

Project Description

First Month

Investigate service opportunities or causes to support. If pursuing a service opportunity, determine the following:

- type of service (housing rehabilitation, working at a soup kitchen, volunteering in a hospice, etc.)

- where the service will be performed (on a local, regional, or national level)

- when the service occurs (summer, a weekend, an evening)

- how many young people will participate

If you are going to raise funds to support a good cause, determine what organization you will support, and gather information on the kind of work it does and the people it serves.

Whether performing a service or raising money for an organization, assess the amount of funds you will need to pursue your project, and establish a stock price ($10.00 per share is commonly used).

Develop an application form for the buyer to complete. Be sure to allow spaces for the buyer's name, address, and phone number, and a blank for filling in the number of shares bought (see sample on page 82).

Develop a "stock certificate" to give each stock buyer (see sample on page 83).

Second Month	Publicize the details of the project and extend the invitation to participate in the stock offering. Encourage everyone to "buy stock" from the participating teens, and encourage the teens to sell the stock to family, friends, co-workers, classmates, and parishioners.

To publicize, use whatever means of communication are available to you in your parish and community. Some common means are the following:

- parish newsletter
- bulletin
- parish mailing
- announcements
- posters and flyers
- parish website

Each stockholder should complete an application form and be given a stock certificate.

Third Month

Once the stock sale is completed, publish a listing of the stockholders, utilizing some or all of the publicity outlets you have.

After the project is completed or the donation made, organize a stockholders' dinner or breakfast. The meal can be a simple pancake breakfast or spaghetti dinner or something more elaborate that reflects the culture of the people who have been served.

After the meal, share information and memories from the service experience, using slides, witness talks, and prayer. If the funds were donated to an organization or cause, share information regarding the organization by distributing pamphlets and photos, or by inviting a representative from the organization to address the group regarding the work of the organization.

Special Considerations

If the necessary amount of money for the service experience is large, the Stock Sale might be just one of a number of fund raisers.

If your group engages in a service experience outside of your area, an on-site photo or a postcard should be sent to each stockholder.

Results

Involving the entire parish results in a broader base of ownership in the service experience. Everyone feels a part of it, not only the young people who actually perform the service. Elderly parishioners who cannot physically help are still a great part of the project when they sponsor a young person.

Reflection

The Stock Sale is an excellent way to raise funds without involving a lot of work or expense. The sale encourages inter-generational sharing, and the postcards and photos sent home during the service project help to build relationships across generations.

Remarks

Twelve young people and adults from St. Mary Magdalene Parish in Waupaca, WI, attended a Catholic Heart Workcamp in Minnesota. Although this was the first Stock Sale by the parish youth, they raised over $1,000 in a parish that has 1,000 families.

Adapted from project by

Betty Manion
Director of Religious Education
St. Mary Magdalene Parish
Waupaca, WI

Important Announcement from the
SMM Stock Clearing House

Don't miss out on this once-a-year opportunity to purchase shares of stock in the SMM Summer Service Trip! This year, eleven SMM students are hoping to participate in the Catholic Heart Workcamp in the Twin Cities. For only $10.00 per share, you can help fund their trip and ensure their participation.

Stockholder benefits include receiving a minimum of one (1) postcard from a participating student while at the Workcamp in Minnesota. Each Stockholder will also be invited to a Fall Stockholder's Dinner, where slides and stories of the Workcamp Experience will be shared by the students.

Remember, this is a one-time offer and stock shares can be bought ONLY by returning the completed application form at the bottom of this announcement. You will receive your stock certificate in the mail and you will be notified of the Fall Stockholder's Dinner.

Hurry, and participate in this worthwhile and exciting offer!

. . . .

Application Form

Yes! I would like to become a SMM "Heartcamp" stockholder. Enclosed please find my payment of $_____ for _____share(s) of stock at $10.00 per share. *(Please make checks payable to St. Mary Magdalene Parish.)*

Name _____

Address_____

City_____State_____ZIP_____Phone _____

Mail this form, along with your payment to:

The Saint Mary Magdalene Youth
Catholic Heart Workcamp Stock Sale
123 Your Street
Your Town, State, Postal Code

Thank you for your support of our Summer Service Trip!

SMM Stock Clearing House

This certificate entitles [N] to _____ shares of stock in the Saint Mary Magdalene Youth Summer Service Trip and to all benefits of this program as stated in the application form.*

Signed _____ Date _____

Chairperson

SMM Stock Clearing House

Collect additional dividends at the Heavenly Gates.

"Let the little children come to me...

for it is to such as these that the kingdom of heaven belongs."

Matthew 19:14

Vacation Bible School for Children

Purpose of Project

To provide high school youth with an opportunity to serve the children of homeless families, who are often forgotten or absorbed into the activities of their parent or parents. This Vacation Bible School project allows "kids to be kids" and "kids to help kids."

Scripture References

Matthew 19:14

Jesus said, "Let the little children come to me, and do not stop them; for it is to such as these that the kingdom of heaven belongs."

Matthew 7:11

If you then, who are evil, know how to give good gifts to your children, how much more will your Father in heaven give good things to those who ask him!"

Mark 7:27

He said to her, "Let the children be fed first, for it is not fair to take the children's food and throw it to the dogs."

Catholic Social Teachings

Mother and Teacher [74]
(Mater et Magistra)
Pope John XXIII, 1961

The economic prosperity of a nation is not so much its total assets in terms of wealth and property, as the equitable division and distribution of this wealth. This it is which guarantees the personal development of the members of society, which is the true goal of a nation's economy.

Peace on Earth [53]
(Pacem et Terris)
Pope John XXIII, 1963

Individual citizens and intermediate groups are obliged to make their specific contributions to the common welfare. One of the chief consequences of this is that they must bring their own interests into harmony with the needs of the community, and must contribute their goods and their services as civil authorities have prescribed, in accord with the norms of justice and within the limits of their competence.

On Social Concern [39]
(Sollicitudo Rei Socialis)
Pope John Paul II, 1987

Those who are more influential, because they have a greater share of goods and common services, should feel responsible for the weaker and be ready to share with them all they possess...The church feels called to take her stand beside the poor, to discern the justice of their requests, and to help satisfy them, without losing sight of the good of groups in the context of the common good.

Communities Involved

High school students and the children of families who live, at least temporarily, in a shelter for the homeless or abused.

Project Time Line

- Begin preparations in March.
- One month prior to the Vacation Bible School, hold a parish drive for cleaning supplies, diapers, baby wipes, paper towels, etc.
- Continue the drive throughout the summer and donate the items to the shelter.

Project Description

Make personal contact with the supervisor of the shelter to secure permission for the week-long Vacation Bible School. Be prepared to give a detailed description of what will take place, what will be involved, and the expectations of the groups involved.

Publicize in the parish or school to inform the youth of this opportunity for leadership development and Christian service. Send letters, permission slips, medical release forms, and contact information to all youths in grades 9-12. Follow up with those who indicate an interest and register them for the project.

Meet with all adults and youths who will be involved. Provide training, if necessary, and arrange for any supplies you will need.

Develop a schedule for each morning of the school. A suggested schedule follows:

8:30 a.m.—Gather adults and youth leaders for prayer and review of morning plans.

9:00 a.m.—Breakfast
Serve a simple breakfast such as fresh fruit, juice, and bread. Keep a happy, spirited conversation going to set the tone for the day. Have on hand crayons and coloring books (with religious art preferably) to occupy the children who finish eating before the others.

9:30 a.m.—Prayer Time
Begin with prayer, and include all petitions that are voiced by the children (and any parents in attendance). Also pray for family members who live in separate locations, for work, for guidance, etc.

9:45 a.m.—Opening Story

Focus on a specific story from the life of Jesus each day. Stories can be taken from a children's Bible. Suggestions include the story of Zacchaeus (Luke 19:2-10), the multiplication of the loaves and fish (Matthew 14:15-21), and Peter receiving the ministry blessing from Jesus (Matthew 16:13-19).

10:00 a.m.—Craft Time

For the crafts, the high schoolers help the younger children on a one-to-one basis. Crafts might include activities like the following:

- prayer beads—string craft beads on a leather string and tie a knot between each bead. Each bead can represent a different prayer intention (for family, for the world, for peace, etc.)

- refrigerator fish—decorate a clip art fish with watercolors and attach it to a refrigerator magnet. The fish are reminders of the many gifts that Jesus shares with us when we believe in him.

- Jesus stones—write the word Jesus on stones and shellac the surface. The stones can be used in times of prayer.

- prayer chain—join construction paper loops together to form a 14-day prayer experience centering on the needs of each person.

10:30 a.m.—Outside Break

Weather permitting, plan an outside activity at this time. Interactive games such as "red light, green light" and "Simon Says" are always popular.

The younger children of the shelter (ages 2-4) might enjoy riding their playground tricycles around during this time (allowing them to "show-off" for their leaders).

Encourage the children to use their creativity, using chalk to draw a scene on the sidewalk about the Bible story they heard that morning. This can be a visual reminder all day for them of the lesson Jesus wanted them to learn.

11:00 a.m.—Story time with reflection

Another Bible story is shared and children are encouraged to share what they learn or hear in the story.

11:30 a.m.—Closing Prayer

End the morning with spontaneous prayer. Ask the children to call out the names of people or things for which they are thankful. Everyone should respond, "We Thank You Lord!"

11:45 a.m.—Clean Up

12:00 noon—Team Lunch

Evaluate the morning with the team while sharing lunch. Make final plans for the next day.

12:30 p.m.—Departure

Option: On the last day of the VBS, it is fun to plan a cookout of hot dogs, fresh vegetables, and watermelon for the children and their parents.

Special Considerations

A shelter that ministers to mothers/fathers with children or families is needed. Transportation is the responsibility of the youth involved in the Vacation Bible School, or group transportation via bus or van will need to be arranged. If possible, get needed resources and supplies from the existing supply center in the parish religious education or youth ministry offices. Additional materials such as buckets of sidewalk chalk and crayons and coloring books will need to be donated or purchased.

Results

Parish youth are able to see a wider church through this service activity. The city, town, or village becomes a bit smaller. Youth are able to put a name, a face, and an emotion with the issues of poverty, discrimination, and hopelessness. The expectations are generally exceeded. Youth often continue to discuss the children by name long after the VBS is over. The children become part of them and are remembered in their prayers.

Reflection

Each participant is encouraged to submit a reflection to be shared with members of the parish. In the daily evaluation, the youth are encouraged to share what an impact the VBS is having on their own spiritual lives. Deep and thoughtful sharing is part of the evaluation.

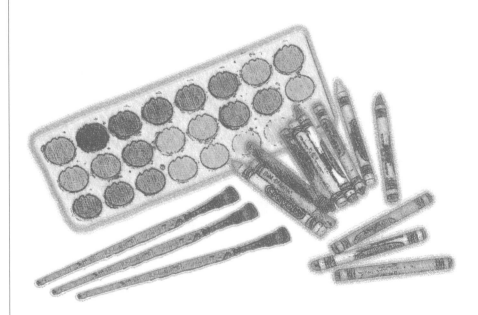

Additional Advice

- Be flexible. The population and age of children in any shelter can change daily. Be prepared to work with two or twenty children on a moment's notice. Also, the age range can change in a day!

- Be sensitive. We assumed that the children would have breakfast before starting each day, but they literally got out of bed, got dressed, and came to the table to participate.

- Take people where they are! Jesus was a foreign concept to many of the children. We may take our faith for granted but our brothers and sisters at the shelter may need us to share at a very basic level.

Remarks

"Our children desperately needed this type of attention. The youth from St. Agnes Parish came with such enthusiasm to serve! Thank you for giving of yourselves so freely. God bless you!"
Marguerite J.— House Supervisor, St. Vincent de Paul Society

"Will you all be back next week?"
Beth Ann—a mother of two at the shelter

Submitted by

Ellen Mommaerts, Youth Minister
Deacon Bob Nooker, Director of Religious Education
St. Agnes Parish
Green Bay, WI

Videos to Go!

Purpose of Project

Involve young people in outreach to the elderly and homebound in a parish or community. Using their own gifts and talents, the teens are able to share the "Good News" through video.

Scripture References
1 Timothy 4:12-16

Let no one despise your youth, but set the believers an example in speech and conduct, in love, in faith, in purity. Until I arrive, give attention to the public reading of scripture, to exhorting, to teaching. Do not neglect the gift that is in you, which was given to you through prophecy with the laying on of hands by the council of elders. Put these things into practice, devote yourself to them, so that all may see your progress. Pay close attention to yourself and to your teaching; continue in these things, for in doing this you will save both yourself and your hearers.

Catholic Social Teachings
A Call to Action [10]
(Octogesima Adveniens)
Pope Paul VI, 1971

[Humanity] is experiencing a new loneliness; it is not in the face of a hostile nature which it has taken... centuries to subdue, but in an anonymous crowd which surrounds [men and women] and in which [they feel themselves to be strangers]. Urbanization, undoubtedly an irreversible stage in the development of human societies, confronts [humanity] with difficult problems. How [are we] to master its growth, regulate its organization, and successfully accomplish its animation for the good of all?

Communities Involved

Young people in the parish and the elderly and homebound.

Project Time Line

It takes approximately five weeks, or sessions, to complete this project.

Project Description
Week 1

Meet with the adult leaders—catechists, teachers, or youth minister—to establish background for discussion with the young participants, and to review a proposed time line. The teens will be making a videotape of a dramatization of a Bible story (or several stories). They will wear costumes and need props and background music. It is important that the young people recognize that the homebound, ill, or elderly have a "connection" with the parish. Young people with their energy, enthusiasm, and life bring joy to the elderly and homebound.

Week 2	Each group will need a play or skit to perform. An original script can be written, or use a published resource. (See a sample play on pages 93-95. Additional resource suggestions are given on page 92.) The adult group leader should read the play with the young people and provide guidance as they select roles, determine the set design and scenery, identify the needed props and music, and decide on a camera person (a student can usually do this).

When everyone is assigned a task, begin working. Decide who should wear what and where they might get the clothing and props. Select appropriate music. Provide a cassette player to tape the different sounds you'll need. |
Week 3	Work on the scenery and rehearse the skits.
Week 4	Hold dress rehearsal, and make a final tape. Make arrangements for duplicating the tapes.
Week 5	View the final tape with the participants so that they can see their work! Make greeting cards and notes of explanation to go along with the videos (also see *Reflection*). Make arrangements to get the videos delivered.

Special Considerations

Contact the parish office for the names and addresses of the elderly of the parish and/or community. Special arrangements may need to be made for those who do not have access to a TV and VCR.

Results

Participants reported they "really got into" this project and had fun doing it. Responses from those receiving a video tape were delightful.

Reflection

The project should be thoroughly explained to the recipients of the videos in order to avoid any confusion. In addition to speaking with them about the project, enclose in each greeting card a simple, printed explanation of the project, as well as a short summary of the bible story on which each skit is based.

Remarks

If you have more than one skit, have the same camera person videotape all of them. Put all skits on one tape.

Actors and actresses may need to be reminded to practice their parts and speak loudly and clearly. Scenery can be made with things that can be found at home. Costumes and music should reflect the theme and the time.

Be certain that the camera battery is charged!

Some sources for plays and skits are Treehaus Publishing (513-683-5716), Group Publishing (800-447-1070), Twenty-Third Publications (800-321-0411).

Adapted from project by

Jane Angha
St. Paul Parish
Combined Locks, WI

Videos to Go!

Death of Lazarus
JOHN 11

Messenger Jesus! Jesus! I have a message for you from Mary and Martha. Their brother Lazarus is very sick!

Jesus His sickness won't end in death. It will bring glory to God and to God's son.

Storyteller Jesus loved Martha and her sister and her brother. But he stayed where he was for two more days.

Jesus *(speaking to the disciples)*
Now we will go back to Judea.

Disciple 1 Teacher, the people there want to stone you to death! Why do you want to go back?

Jesus *(speaking to the disciples)*
Aren't there twelve hours in each day? If you walk during the day, you will have light from the sun, and you won't stumble. But if you walk during the night, you will stumble, because you don't have any light.

Our friend Lazarus is asleep, and I am going there to wake him up.

Disciple 2 Lord, if he is asleep, he will get better.

Jesus Lazarus is dead! I am glad that I wasn't there, because now you will have a chance to put your faith in me. Let's go to him.

Thomas Come on. Let's go, so we can die with him.

Storyteller It was not good. When Jesus was nearing his friends, he heard that Lazarus had already died. As Jesus walked into the village, Martha ran out to meet him.

Martha	Lord, if you had been here, my brother would not have died. Yet even now I know that God will do anything you ask.
Jesus	Martha, your brother will live again.
Martha	I know he will be raised up again on the last day, when all the dead are raised.
Jesus	I am the one who raises the dead to life! Everyone who has faith in me will live, even if they die. And everyone who lives because of faith in me will never really die. Do you believe this?
Martha	Yes, Lord! I believe that you are Christ, the Son of God. You are the one we hoped would come into the world.
Martha	*(running back home to speak to Mary)* Mary, the Teacher is here, and he wants to see you.
Storyteller	Well, when Mary heard this, she left the house quickly to meet Jesus who was still outside the village. Those who came to comfort Mary followed her, thinking that she was going to Lazarus' tomb.
Mary	*(at Jesus' feet, crying)* Lord, if you had been here, my brother would not have died.
Jesus	*(upset by everyone's crying)* Where have you put his body?
Crowd	Lord, come and you will see.
Onlooker 1	*(seeing Jesus cry)* See how much he loved Lazarus.
Onlooker 2	*(speaking to others in the crowd)* He gives sight to the blind. Why couldn't he have kept Lazarus from dying?
Storyteller	Clearly Jesus was upset. He went to the grave site and asked the people to roll away the stone at the entrance of the tomb.

Martha   *(realizing what Jesus was doing)*
Lord, you know that Lazarus has been dead four days, and there will be a bad smell.

Jesus   Didn't I tell you that if you had faith, you would see the glory of God?

(after the stone had been rolled away, and looking up to heaven)
Father, I thank you for answering my prayer. I know that you always answer my prayers. But I said this, so that the people here would believe that you sent me.

(Jesus paused and then shouted into the tomb)
Lazarus, come out!

Storyteller   Well, a man came out bound in strips of cloth from head to foot.

Jesus   Untie him and let him go.

ADDITIONAL RESOURCES FOR YOUTH MINISTERS

Pflaum Publishing Group's Youth Ministry Resource Library

Developed and teen-tested by experienced, dedicated catechists, these creative new resources engage and involve teens. Each is 96 pages, 8½" x 11," perfect bound. Reproducible handouts are included as needed.

Getting Started: 100 Icebreakers for Youth Gatherings
Help young people get comfortable with one another, facilitate sharing and discussion, and build a sense of community—while having a lot of fun!

Making Connections: 25 Stories for Sharing Faith with Teens
Initiate and guide meaningful discussion by teens on a wide choice of current topics, such as • computer chat rooms • depression • pornography • cheating • evangelizing.

Prayer Services for Teens: 34 Resources for Special Reasons and Church Seasons
Let teens lead their peers in prayer; these simple, yet powerful, prayer services make it work! Themes revolve around Feast Days and Holidays, Advent and Lent, and Life Circumstances.

Conversations with Teens
CATHOLIC PERSPECTIVES

Everything you need for a complete session on any of eight themes. Straightforward, easy-to-follow directions for the leader, including background from Church teachings and suggestions for parent involvement. The session itself includes icebreakers, faith-sharing stories, suggestions for service, activities, games, and prayer experiences. Each is 16 pages, 8½" x 11." Reproducible handouts are included as needed.

Keep all eight topics on hand, and choose the one that fits your needs when you need it.

- The Death Penalty
- Family Crises
- Serving Others
- Forgiveness & Healing
- Dealing with Emotions
- Respect for Others
- Dealing with Death
- Sexuality

To order, or for more information, call Pflaum Publishing Group at 1-800-543-4383.